Asian American Women and Men

THE GENDER LENS:
A Sage Publications / Pine Forge Press Series

Series Editors

Judith A. Howard
University of Washington

Barbara Risman
North Carolina State University

Mary Romero
Arizona State University

Joey Sprague
University of Kansas

Books in the Series

Yen Le Espiritu, *Asian American Women and Men: Labor, Laws, and Love*

Judith A. Howard and Jocelyn A. Hollander, *Gendered Situations, Gendered Selves: A Gender Lens on Social Psychology*

Books Forthcoming

Francesca Cancian and Stacy Oliker, *A Gendered View of Care*

Scott Coltrane, *Gender and Families*

Patricia Yancey Martin and David Collinson, *The Gendered Organization*

Judith Lorber, *Gender, Health, and Illness*

Pepper Schwartz and Virginia Rutter, *Gender, Sex, and Society*

Asian American Women and Men

Labor, Laws, and Love

YEN LE ESPIRITU
University of California, San Diego

SAGE PUBLICATIONS
Thousand Oaks ■ London ■ New Delhi

For information address:

Sage Publications, Inc.
2455 Teller Road
Thousand Oaks, California 91320
E-mail: order@sagepub.com

SAGE Publications Ltd.
6 Bonhill Street
London EC2A 4PU
United Kingdom

SAGE Publications India Pvt. Ltd.
M-32 Market
Greater Kailash I
New Delhi 110 048 India

Printed in the United States of America

Library of Congress Cataloging-in-Publication Data

Espiritu, Yen Le, 1963-
    Asian American women and men: Labor, laws, and love / Yen Le Espiritu.
        p.   cm.—(Gender lens; vol. 1)
    Includes bibliographical references (p.) and index.
    ISBN 0-8039-7254-7 (cloth: acid-free paper).—ISBN
0-8039-7255-5 (pbk.: acid-free paper)
    1. Asian Americans—Social conditions. I. Title. II. Series.
E184.O6E875   1996
305.895073—dc20   96-10123

This book is printed on acid-free paper that meets Environmental Protection Agency standards for recycled paper.

97 98 99 00 01 02 03 10 9 8 7 6 5 4 3 2 1

Acquiring Editor: Peter Labella
Production Editor: Diana E. Axelsen
Designer: Lisa S. Mirski
Desktop Typesetter: Andrea D. Swanson
Cover Designer: Lisa S. Mirski
Print Buyer: Anna Chin

C O N T E N T S

CHAPTER 1

Labor, Laws, and Love 1

CHAPTER 2

Stretching Gender, Family, and Community Boundaries, 1840s-1930s 16

CHAPTER 6

Beyond Dualisms: Constructing an Imagined Community... 108

To my mother,
the source of my strength

It is now over 20 years since feminist sociologist have identified gender as an important analytic dimension in sociology. In the intervening two decades, theory and research on gender have grown exponentially. With this series, we intend to further this scholarship, as well as ensure that theory and research on gender become fully integrated into the discipline as a whole.

Beth Hess and Myra Marx Ferree, in *Analyzing Gender* (1988), identified three stages in the study of women and men since 1970. Initially, the emphasis was on sex differences and the extent to which such differences might be based in biological properties of individuals. In the second stage, the focus shifted to individual-level sex roles and socialization, exposing gender as the product of specific social arrangements, although still conceptualizing it as an individual trait. The hallmark of the third stage is the recognition of the centrality of gender as an organizing principle in all social systems, including work, politics, everyday interaction, families, economic development, law, education, and a host of other social domains. As our understanding of gender has become more social, so has our awareness that gender is experienced and organized in race- and class-specific ways.

In the summer of 1992 the American Sociological Association funded a small conference, organized by Barbara Risman and Joey Sprague, to discuss the evolution of gender in these distinctly sociological frameworks. The conference brought together a sampling of gender scholars working in a wide range of substantive areas with a diversity of methods to focus on gender as a principle of social organization. The discussions of the state of feminist scholarship made it clear that gender is pervasive in society and operates at multiple levels. Gender shapes identities and perception, interactional practices, and the very forms of social institutions, and it does so in race- and class-specific ways. If we did not see gender in social phenomena, we were not seeing clearly.

The participants in this ASA-sponsored seminar recognized that although these developing ideas about gender were widely accepted by feminist sociologists and many others who study social inequalities, they were relatively unfamiliar to many who work within other sociological paradigms. This book series was conceived at that conference as a means to introduce these ideas to sociological colleagues and students, and to help further develop gender scholarship.

As series editors, we feel it is time for gender scholars to speak to our colleagues and to the general education of students. There are many sociologists and scholars in other social sciences who want to incorporate scholarship on gender and its intersections with race, class, and sexuality in their teaching and research, but lack the tools to do so. For those who have not worked in this area, the prospect of the bibliographic research necessary to develop supplementary units, or to transform their own teaching and scholarship, is daunting. Moreover, the publications necessary to penetrate a curriculum resistant to change and encumbered by inertia have simply not been available. We conceptualize this book series as a way of meeting the needs of these scholars, and thereby also encouraging the development of the sociological understanding of gender by offering a "Gender Lens."

What do we mean by a "gender lens"? It means working to make gender visible in social phenomena, asking if, how, and why social processes, standards, and opportunities differ systematically for women and men. It also means recognizing that gender inequality is inextricably braided with other systems of inequity. Looking at the world through a gendered lens thus implies two seemingly contradictory tasks. First, it means unpacking the taken-for-granted assumptions about gender that pervade sociological research, and social life more generally. At the same time, looking through a gender lens means showing just how central assumptions about gender continue to be to the organization of the social world, regardless of their empirical reality. We show how our often unquestioned ideas about gender affect the worlds we see, the questions we ask, the answers we can envision. The *Gender Lens* series is committed to social change directed toward eradicating these inequalities. Our goals are consistent with initiatives at colleges and universities across the United States that are encouraging the development of more diverse scholarship and teaching.

The books in the *Gender Lens* series are aimed at different audiences and have been written for a variety of uses, from assigned readings in introductory undergraduate courses to graduate seminars, and as professional resources for our colleagues. The series includes several different styles of books that address these goals in distinct ways. We are excited about this series and anticipate that it will have an enduring impact on the direction of both pedagogy and scholarship in sociology and other related social sciences. We invite you, the reader, to join us in thinking through these difficult but exciting issues by offering feedback or developing your own project and proposing it to us for the series.

About This Volume

The current volume presents a gendered analysis of class, race, ethnicity, and immigration as experienced by Asian American women and men. Conceptualizing Asian Americans from this perspective recognizes gender as an organizing principle in the social system and provides a structure to analyze the relationship between Asian American men and women in the home, community, fields, factories, offices, and in the government.

A sociological perspective of the Asian American experience that is informed by gender not only moves beyond the assimilation model, with its emphasis on cultural determinism, but gives voice to women as active agents working, struggling, triumphing, and living with men. In *Asian American Women and Men: Labor, Laws, and Love,* Yen Espiritu analyzes how race, gender, and class simultaneously shape the relations between Asian American men and women by drawing from a wide range of interdisciplinary research and writings in sociology, as well as Asian American Studies, Ethnic Studies, Women's Studies, and Cultural Studies. Unlike traditional sociological work on Asian Americans, Espiritu does not privilege "whiteness" but approaches her work by placing the history, interpersonal experiences, and the concerns of Asian Americans at the center.

Espiritu focuses on immigration, labor, and ideology, analyzing the race- and gender-based immigration policies and labor conditions that men and women confronted in the United States and that structures their subordinate place in the patriarchal economy. The historical oppression of Asian American men and women draws attention to the relationship between social structure and culture, challenging dominant cultural explanations about the Chinese, Japanese, Filipino, and other Asian experience in the United States. Immigration policies not only shaped migration and settlement of Asian men and women but also reconfigured gender relations and their relative positions of power and states in the United States. Policies regulating who migrated and where affected the demographics within Asian communities and had long-term impacts on interpersonal relationships between men and women. Asian American men and women enter a labor market that is racially and sexually segregated. Labor conditions affect family life by requiring women to engage in paid labor and domestic labor, some-times to compensate for men's low wages, at other times to replace wages in a labor market discriminating against Asian men. Espiritu examines the impact that women's wages had on family and commu-nity relationships, contributing to both gender equality and the preser-vation of male privilege. She concludes her examination of Asian Ameri-can men and women by examining ideological racism, particularly representations of gender and sexuality constructed in the process of racial domination.

We hope this book and others in the *Gender Lens* series will help the reader develop his and her own gender lens to better and more accurately understand our social environments. As sociologists, we believe that an accurate understanding of inequality is a prerequisite for effective social change.

Judith A. Howard
Barbara Risman
Mary Romero
Joey Sprague
Gender Lens Series Editors

ACKNOWLEDGMENTS

This book was written during the worst and best of times. The worst of times because it began soon after the death of my beloved stepfather. With his death, I lost not only a parent but also a teacher, a listener, a friend—and most of all, an avid fan of any and all of my undertakings. He, a white American; I, a Vietnamese refugee—somehow, we connected. He was the first one to teach me English, the first to point out that I had a sense of humor, and the first to show me the importance and possibilities of cross-racial relationships—and thus it was to him that I dedicated my first book, *Asian American Panethnicity*. Though he is now gone, his wisdom, gentle guidance, and unbending faith in my abilities continue to inform this and my subsequent projects.

But this book also came into being during the best of times—amidst the enthusiasm and support of many groups and individuals. It is part of the Gender Lens book series, a wonderful collaborative project that attends to both the theory and praxis aspects of feminist scholarship. I am grateful to Mary Romero, my project *madrina*, for inviting me to write this book and for providing the necessary support along the way. I thank Peter Labella for his effective stewardship, Judith Howard for her generous praise of and insightful comments on the final draft, and the other series editors for their comments on various drafts of the manuscript. I also want to acknowledge Luana Ross, Donna Hughes, Joyce Chinen, and Wendy Ng for joining me at a brainstorm session at the 1995 meeting of the American Sociological Association.

This book also benefits much from the insights provided by the students in my Race, Gender, and Class course (ES 183) that I taught at the University of California, San Diego (UCSD), in the fall of 1995. Committed to the principle that research and teaching should go hand in hand, I purposefully scheduled myself to teach this course during the final stage of my writing. I wanted to be able to combine my day and night jobs: to share with the students during the day what I had just written the previous night and to incorporate their comments, questions, and criticisms into the manuscript. And that was the way it worked out: Through our passionate and compassionate class discussions, the students challenged me to develop a deeper understanding of the interworkings of race, class, and gender. This class confirms for me the importance of teaching at a public university, where students from diverse ethnic, racial, and class backgrounds meet to provide each other the needed tools to better comprehend power relations in U.S. society. It also deepens my appreciation for my colleagues in the Ethnic Studies Department at UCSD—a supportive group of people who acknowledge each other's achievements, respect each other's work, and take seriously their charge to be "educators."

I also owe much to Asian American studies scholars who have long struggled to correct histories, create new bodies of knowledge, and open spaces in the academy for younger scholars. This book profits from this collective history and from the important contributions of scholars such as Sucheng Chan, Evelyn Nakano Glenn, Elaine Kim, Lisa Lowe, Gary Okihiro, and Paul Ong. Finally, this book would not have been written without the love and support of my husband, Abe, and the much-appreciated distractions provided by our two daughters, Evyn and Maya. Most of all, this book is for my mother, a spirited woman who strives under adverse conditions. Her no-nonsense approach to life hones my problem-solving skills, and her selfless nature teaches me to take seriously my responsibilities in life. But above all, I am impressed by her strength—the type of strength that propelled her to take driving lessons, just 2 days after the death of my father, so that she could soon take over his responsibility of picking up my children after school. It is to her gentleness, selflessness, and strength that this book is dedicated.

CHAPTER 1

Labor, Laws, and Love

This book is about labor, laws, and love. It explores how racist and gendered labor conditions and immigration laws have affected relations between Asian American men and women. The first goal is to document how the historical and contemporary oppression of Asian Americans has (re)structured the balance of power between Asian American men and women and shaped their struggles to create and maintain social institutions and systems of meaning. The larger goal is to show how race, gender, and class, as categories of difference, do not parallel but instead intersect and confirm each other. Few existing works explore the experiences of Asian Americans from a gendered perspective. The few that do are concerned primarily with explicating the relationship between Asian American feminists and white feminists or between Asian American women and white men (see Chan, 1989, p. 22; Cheung, 1990, p. 235).[1] Both tendencies have the effect of recentering white men and white women. As a point of departure, this book spotlights the long-neglected issue of relations between Asian American women and men.

Foreground and Background:
Sociology and Asian American Studies

Asian American activist Glenn Omatsu (1991) reminded us that "whatever conceptual framework we choose, . . . we need to constantly remind ourselves that each framework is selective. It serves to bring certain issues to the foreground while pushing others into the background" (p. 80). Between 1920 and 1960, Robert Park's conception of the "race relations cycle"—competition, conflict, accommodation, and assimilation—dominated thinking about Asians (and other groups of color) in the United States (Yu, 1995). In a critical review of the sociological studies

1

on Chinese Americans, Lucie Cheng Hirata (1976) reported that through the 1950s, the majority of writings on Chinese Americans cited the work of Robert Park or assumed assimilation to be the final outcome. In the 1960s, Milton Gordon's refinement of the assimilation concept formed the theoretical base for many studies on Chinese and Japanese Americans (Hirata, 1976, p. 23). This conceptual framework foregrounded questions relating to the cultural traits or behavioral patterns of Asians but pushed into the background questions concerning economic exploitation, institutional discrimination, and other systems of power in U.S. society. These sociological studies also ignored the experiences of women or subsumed them under those of men. For example, in an oft-cited study of ethnic businesses among Chinese and Japanese immigrants, sociologist Ivan Light (1972) relegated Asian women (when included) to the institution of family but failed to report that the labor of the women had been indispensable to the establishment and success of the family enterprises.

Emerging from the student and community grassroots movements of the late 1960s and the early 1970s, Asian American studies, an alternative field of study that "link[s] formal knowledge and history with community and political engagement" (Leong, 1995, p. vii), contests the cultural and racial bias of the assimilationist framework. Like other ethnic studies programs, Asian American studies challenges the prevailing academic power structure, particularly its claims to objectivity and universalism (Hu-DeHart, 1993). Foregrounding race and racism, Asian American studies critiques dominant U.S. ideologies such as the claim of equal opportunity and calls attention instead to the persistence of inequality in the United States. Though important, this anti-racism agenda has homogenized differences among Asian Americans, assuming heterosexuality and subordinating issues of gender and social class (Hune, 1995; Yanagisako, 1995). Asian American history was normalized as masculine, with women's experiences, contributions, and standpoints omitted, distorted, discounted, or rendered invisible (Okihiro, 1994, p. 65). Their omission bolsters the social relations of patriarchy and allows men to "institute and maintain a system of repression and privilege" (Okihiro, 1994, p. xii). Along the same lines, early Asian American cultural nationalism pursued an aggressively masculinist agenda "to challenge the metonymic equation of Asian with the feminine" (Yanagisako, 1995, p. 287). Confronted with a history of painful "emasculation," these male writers took whites to task for their racist myths but were often blind to their own acceptance of the racialized patriarchal construct of gender stereotypes (Cheung, 1990, pp. 236-237).

Challenging this male-centered perspective, Asian American women, both inside and outside the academy, began to uncover their "buried past" and recover their muted voices and, in so doing, to push their experiences into the foreground. They recorded the public and domestic lives of Asian American women (Cheng, 1984; Glenn, 1986; Yu, 1989), charted the development and progress of Asian American feminism (Chen, 1976; Chow, 1987; Ling, 1989), and spotlighted the cultural production of Asian American women (Ling, 1990). In the process, Asian American women emerged as active agents who shaped their own lives and not as objects excluded or acted on by others. Needless to say, the inclusion of women on "those pages of paper" (Okihiro, 1994, p. 66) has produced a truer account of the Asian American collective past. On the other hand, because its mission is to recenter women—to make their worldviews and experiences more visible and central in the construction of knowledge—these accounts of Asian American women have made relatively little attempt to integrate the women's experiences into gendered accounts of Asian American life (Chan, 1989, p. 22; Gabaccia, 1992, p. xv). That is, they have not explored the way(s) in which gender, as an organizing principle in social systems, structures the relationship between Asian American men and women in different social domains. In an analysis of the narrative structure and content of "Asian American history" as it was being taught in the late 1980s in several major West Coast universities, Sylvia Yanagisako (1995) reported that although all the Asian American studies courses she examined included some materials on Asian American women, these readings "tend to avoid the issue of sexual inequality *among* Asian Americans" (p. 282).

Reading the experiences of Asian Americans from a gendered perspective, this book foregrounds the patriarchal system(s) that produces power differentials between Asian American men and women. But as Robyn Wiegman (1991) pointed out, patriarchy is constitutive of more than gender difference (p. 311). That is, gender differentiation and oppression is not a universal experience but is structured differently, depending on how it intersects with other inequalities such as race and class. Accordingly, this book examines the *simultaneity* of the impact of race, gender, and class exploitation on relations between Asian American men and women.

Theorizing Race, Gender, and Class

Almost a quarter of a century ago, when "second-wave" feminist scholars identified gender as an important aspect of social organization, they pronounced that traditional scholarship represented the experiences of men as gender neutral, making it unnecessary to deal with women. With men's lives assumed to be the norm, women's experiences were subsumed under those of men, narrowly categorized, or excluded altogether (Weinberg, 1992, p. 4). Responding to the omission of women, the feminist agenda at the time was to fill in gaps, correct sexist biases, and create new topics out of women's experiences. In the next stage, feminist thinking advanced from woman-centered analyses to providing a "gendered" understanding of sociological phenomena—one that traced the significance of gender organization and relations in all institutions and in shaping men's as well as women's lives. The feminist agenda shifted then from advocating the inclusion of women to transforming the basic conceptual and theoretical frameworks of the field.

In a 1985 statement on the treatment of gender in research, the American Sociological Association's Committees on the Status of Women in Sociology (1985) urged members of the profession "to explicitly acknowledge the social category of gender, and gender differences in power, at each step of the research process" (p. 1). But a gendered transformation of knowledge has yet to take place in sociology. In a review essay, Judith Stacey and Barrie Thorne (1985) argued that although feminist scholarship has made important contributions to sociology in terms of uncovering and filling gaps in sociological knowledge, it has yet to transform the field. The gender paradigm, which positions gender as a prominent social category creating hierarchies of difference in society, remains a minority position within mainstream sociological paradigms. As in anthropology (Strathorn, 1987) and history (Weinberg, 1992), feminist sociology seems to have been "both co-opted and ghettoized, while the discipline as a whole and its dominant paradigms have proceeded relatively unchanged" (Stacey & Thorne, 1985, p. 302). The use of gender as a variable, conceptualized in terms of sex difference rather than as a central theoretical concept, is a prime example of the co-optation of feminist perspectives (Stacey & Thorne, 1985, p. 308). In a more recent review of the field, Sylvia Pedraza (1991) similarly concluded that within sociology, "A truly gendered understanding of most topics has not been achieved" (p. 305).

Although the concept of gender is invaluable, the gender process cannot be understood independently of class and race. Class and gender overlap when the culture of patriarchy enables capitalists to benefit from the exploitation of the labor of both men and women. Because patriarchy mandates that men serve as good financial providers, it obliges them to toil in the exploitative capitalist wage market (Hondagneu-Sotelo, 1994, p. 188). Correspondingly, the patriarchal assumption that women are not the breadwinners—and therefore can afford to work for less—allows employers to justify hiring women at lower wages and under poorer working conditions. On the other hand, in however limited a way, wage employment affords women a measure of economic and personal independence, thus strengthening their claims against patriarchal authority (Okihiro, 1994, p. 91). This is just one of the many contradictions that occur in the interstices of the race/gender/class matrix.

Economic oppression in the United States is not only gendered but also racist. Historically, people of color in the United States have encountered institutionalized economic and cultural racism that has restricted their economic mobility. Due to their gender, race, and noncitizen status, immigrant women of color fare the worst because they are seen as being the most desperate for work at any wage (Hossfeld, 1994, p. 75). Within this racially based social order, there are no gender relations per se, only gender relations as constructed by and between races (Harding, 1991, p. 179). Jane Gaines (1990, p. 198) suggested that insofar as the focus on gender keeps women from seeing other structures of oppression, it functions ideologically in the interests of the dominant group(s). That is, to conceptualize oppression only in terms of male dominance and female subordination is to obscure the centrality of classism, racism, and other forms of inequality in U.S. society (Stacey & Thorne, 1985, p. 311).

Women of color have charged that feminist theory falsely universalizes the category of "woman." As bell hooks (1984) observed, this gender analysis centers on the experiences of white, middle-class women and ignores the way women in different racial groups and social classes experience oppression. For women of color, gender is only part of a larger pattern of unequal social relations. In their daily lives, these women brave not only sexism but also the "entire system of racial and ethnic stratification that defines, stigmatizes, and controls the minority group as a whole" (Healey, 1995, p. 26). These systems of power render irrelevant the public/private distinction for women of color. As Aida Hurtado (1989) reminded us,

> Women of color have not had the benefit of the economic conditions
> that underlie the public/private distinction. . . . Welfare programs and

policies have discouraged family life, sterilization programs have restricted production rights, government has drafted and armed disproportionate numbers of people of color to fight its wars overseas, and
locally, police forces in the criminal justice system arrest and incarcerate
disproportionate numbers of people of color. There is no such thing as
a private sphere for people of color except that which they manage to
create and protect in an otherwise hostile environment. (p. 849)

In this hostile environment, some women of color, in contrast to their
white counterparts, view unpaid domestic work—having children and
maintaining families—more as a form of resistance to racist oppression
than as a form of exploitation by men (Collins, 1990, p. 44; Amott &
Matthaei, 1991, p. 17).

Women of color have also protested their marginalization in traditional feminist scholarship, charging that they have been added to
feminist analysis only "as an afterthought" (Gaines, 1990, p. 201). This
tokenism is evident in the manner in which race has been added to,
rather than integrated into, traditional feminist scholarship. Gaines
(1990, p. 201) pointed out that although feminist anthologies consistently include writings by women of color, the issue of race is conspicu-
ously absent from the rest of the volume. This practice suggests that
white feminists view racism as an issue that affects only people of color
and not as a system that organizes and shapes the daily experiences of
all people. In an anthology of writings by radical women of color,
Cherrie Moraga (1981) recorded her reaction to "dealing with white
women": "I have felt so very dark: dark with anger, with silence, with
the feeling of being walked over" (p. xv). Similarly, Bettie Luke Kan
referred to racism when she explained why Chinese American women
rejected the National Organization of Women: "No matter how hard
you fight to reduce the sexism, when it's all done and over with, you
still have the racism. Because white women will be racist as easily as
their male counterparts. And white women continue to get preferential
treatment over women of color" (cited in Yung, 1986, p. 98). Recentering
race, then, requires feminist scholars to reshape the basic concepts and
theories of their field and to acknowledge that the experiences of white
women and women of color are not just different but connected in
systematic ways (Glenn, 1992, p. 34; Baca Zinn & Dill, 1994, p. 3).

Bringing class and race into the study of gender also requires us to
explicate the positions that white men *and* white women occupy over
men of color. Many white feminists include all males, regardless of color
and social class, into their critique of sexist power relations. This argu-

ment assumes that *any* male in U.S. society benefits from a patriarchal system designed to maintain the unequal relationship that exists between men and women. Pointing to the multiplicities of men's lives, feminists of color have argued that, depending on their race and class, men experience gender differently. Presenting race and gender as relationally constructed, black feminists have referred instead to "racial patriarchy"—a concept that calls attention to the white patriarch/master in American history and his dominance over the black male as well as the black female (Gaines, 1990, p. 202). Providing yet another dimension to the intersections of race and gender, Gaines (1990) pointed out that the "notion of patriarchy is most obtuse when it disregards the position white women occupy over Black men as well as Black women" (p. 202).

Along the same lines, King-Kok Cheung (1990) exhorted white scholars to acknowledge that, like female voices, "the voices of many men of color have been historically silenced or dismissed" (p. 246). The failure of feminist scholarship to theorize the historically specific experiences of men of color makes it difficult for women of color to rally to the feminist cause without feeling divided or without being accused of betrayal (Cheung, 1990, p. 245). As Kimberlee Crenshaw (1989) observed, "Although patriarchy clearly operates within the Black community, . . . the racial context in which Black women find themselves makes the creation of a political consciousness that is oppositional to Black men difficult" (p. 162).

Asian Americans: Their Material and Cultural Lives

Attentive to the intersections of race, class, and gender and to the experiences of both men and women, this book explores how racial patriarchy and class exploitation in the United States have (re)shaped gender relations within the Asian American community. It does so by examining the material and cultural lives of both Asian American women and men over time. Asian American oppression has been most visible in the areas of immigration, labor, and ideology. In this book, I will explicate how racist and gendered immigration policies and labor conditions have worked together to keep Asian Americans in an assigned, subordinate place in the patriarchal economy of U.S. culture. This system of oppression in turn is maintained by a set of "controlling images" that provides the ideological justification for the economic exploitation and social oppression of Asian Americans (see Collins, 1990, p. 67). I will argue that it is this historical oppression of Asian American men and women, along both material and cultural lines, that (re)structures the rules of gender in the Asian American community.

Asian Americans and Immigration

Through the process of migration and settlement, patriarchal relations undergo continual renegotiation as women and men rebuild their lives in the new country. An important task in the study of immigration has been to examine this reconfiguration of gender relations. Theoretically, migration could improve women's social position if it led to increased participation in wage employment, more control over earnings, and greater participation in family decision making (Pessar, 1984). Alternatively, migration might leave gender asymmetries largely unchanged even though certain dimensions of gender inequalities were modified (Curtis, 1986). In a review of the literature on migration and changing gender relations, Marta Tienda and Karen Booth (1991) concluded that there is no consensus about whether migration improves or erodes women's position vis-à-vis men. Instead, past research indicates that migration produces contradictory outcomes whereby women's position is improved in some domains even as it is eroded in others (Morokvasic, 1984). In a recent study of Mexican immigration and settlement, Pierrette Hondagneu-Sotelo (1994) likewise stressed the uneven changes in gender relations, reporting that patriarchal relations do not automatically break down *or* remain intact.

Central to the reconfiguration of gender relations is the change in women's and men's relative positions of power and status in the country of settlement. In general, immigrant men suffer social and economic losses in the transition to life in the United States. When these men are of color, their public status is further eroded due to the racism in U.S. society. Because of the men's losses, the status of immigrant men and women (in terms of relative control of social and economic resources) approaches a situation of greater equality than in the past (Kibria, 1993, p. 8). The rise in women's status relative to that of men erodes men's patriarchal authority in the family and empowers women to challenge that traditional authority (Hondagneu-Sotelo, 1994, pp. 195-196). However, racist and gendered economic exploitation attenuates women's gains. Constrained by their social-structural location in the dominant society, women of color may accept certain components of the traditional patriarchal system to have a strong and intact family—an important bastion of resistance to race and class oppression. In other words, the traditional family, with its admittedly unequal gender relationships, remains one of the few sources of support and of renewal for women and therefore cannot be dismissed (Collins, 1990, p. 44).

For the most part, the literature on migration and gender relations has overlooked the importance of immigration policies in shaping the demographic context within which immigrant men and women have to interact. A high male-to-female sex ratio—a surplus of men over women—can be a source of power for immigrant women who use their comparative scarcity to enhance their status (Guttentag & Secord, 1983). For example, a shortage of women enhances the value of unmarried women in the "marriage market," thus giving these women an immediate kind of power in their relationships with men (Kibria, 1993, p. 121). On the other hand, a surplus of women can contribute to a deterioration of women's position, including the rise of impoverished households headed by single women and the increased exploitation of unskilled migrant workers (Beneria & Roldan, 1987). Asian American lives have been fundamentally shaped by legal exclusions in 1882, 1917, 1924, and 1934, and by the liberalization of immigration laws in 1965.[2] These immigration laws have always been connected to capitalist, racist, and sexist agendas (Mohanty, 1991, pp. 22-26). Lowe (1996) argues that Asian immigration has historically been the site to resolve the contradictions between the U.S. national economy and its political state—between the economic need for cheap and exploitable labor and the political need to constitute a homogeneous nation. Thus, Asian immigrants have been both integrated in the U.S. national economy, its workplaces, and its markets, yet simultaneously marginalized and marked—by immigration restriction and cultural exclusion—as "foreign" and "outside" the national polity. Immigration regulations were also gendered in that female immigrants generally were not accorded their own legal status but were assumed to be "legal appendages of men" (Mohanty, 1991, p. 26). This immigration history suggests that for Asian immigrants and Asian Americans, class struggles have always intersected with and been articulated through race and gender determination (Lowe, 1996).

Prior to World War II, U.S. immigration policies treated Asian male workers primarily as temporary, individual units of labor rather than as members of family groups. Thus, immigration restrictions (and labor recruitment practices) limited the number of female immigrants from Asia. In contrast, in the contemporary period, the dual goals of the 1965 Immigration Act—to facilitate family reunification and to admit skilled workers needed by the U.S. economy—have produced a female-dominated immigrant flow. Although patriarchal practices persisted in both of these periods, the sex ratio in each period influenced the degree to which women were able to modify the traditional gender hierarchies. This book will stress the impacts that changing immigration policies, in conjunction with other structural changes, have had on the lives of Asian American men and women.

Asian Americans and Work

The authority of men over women rests partly on the material resources male workers mobilize in the labor market. In a racist and classist society, most men of color and immigrant men are relegated to the least remunerative and least desirable forms of wage labor. Maxine Baca Zinn and Bonnie Thornton Dill (1994) maintained that labor arrangements are at the core of race, class, and gender inequalities: "Social location in the labor market means that opportunities are influenced by *who* people are—by their being male or female; White, Black, Latina, American Indian, or Asian; rich or poor—rather than what their skills and abilities are" (p. 5). In the United States, racial and colonized minority groups (Native Americans, African Americans, Asian Americans, and Latinos) have historically provided cheap and exploitable sources of labor to meet the needs of the expanding U.S. capitalist economy. Due to their limited access to economic opportunities, men of color experience gender differently from privileged white men. As Elaine Kim (1990) observed, "Asian patriarchy was pushed aside or subsumed by an American patriarchy that did not, because of racism, extend its premise to Asian American men" (p. 75). Similarly, Hondagneu-Sotelo (1994) reported that "Mexican immigrant men's public status in the U.S. is very low, due to racism, insecure and low-paying jobs, and (often) illegal status" (p. 195).

Due to the men's lack of work opportunities, women of color have had to engage in paid labor to make up the income discrepancies (Woo, 1985). At the same time that middle-class white women were being driven into a cult of domesticity, women of color were coping with an extended day, juggling subsistence labor outside the family and domestic labor within it. Thus, the analytical division between productive labor (labor that economically sustains family life) and reproductive labor (labor that reproduces family life), when applied to women of color, must be modified because productive labor is necessary to achieve even minimal levels of family subsistence (Dill, 1994, pp. 164-165). This book will show that most Asian American women, like other women of color, do not separate paid work and housework. Their work outside the home is an extension of their domestic responsibilities, as all family members—women, men, and children—pool their resources to ensure economic subsistence or to propel the family up the economic ladder.

Feminists have long debated the impact of wage earning on the power and status of women. As reviewed by Mirjana Morokvasic (1984), a number of studies indicate that as women become wage workers, they have more economic resources to challenge the authority of men and to fight for a stronger position in the family (pp. 892-893). In her study of Mexican immigrants, Hondagneu-Sotelo (1994) reported that although men still have more status and are more mobile than women, when they migrate they lose power and status in the public sphere, especially in the workplace. As men lose their monopoly of control over resources, they correspondingly lose some of their power and status within the family.

But wage employment also brings losses for women. Although it may give women a greater degree of autonomy in public and private spheres, this gain is often accompanied not only by a heavier workload in the home but also by the exploitation of these women in the workplace (Tienda & Booth, 1991, pp. 54-55). Instead of producing greater sexual equality, the feminization and internationalization of labor has created a new sexual division of labor at the levels of family, community, and nation. Women, particularly immigrant women, constitute an increasingly important but oppressed segment of the world's international labor force. In addition, they face racism and an insecure political and legal status in the country of settlement. Karen Sacks and Nancy Scheper-Hughes (1987) described the multiple oppressions faced by these women: "As immigrants, as members of racial and ethnic minorities, and as women they are oppressed by the racism and sexism of capitalist occupational structures that assign them to marginal and shadow work on the periphery of the national and international economies" (p. 178). As "shadow workers," these women toil in the most exploitative sectors of the economy—in the sweatshops, in domestic service, and in food and cleaning services—performing labor-intensive, low-paying, and physically dangerous work. Given the lack of work opportunities for men in their communities, "These women's participation in even lower-paid wage work [is] a *survival strategy*, a necessity, and *not* a choice" (Sacks & Scheper-Hughes, 1987, pp. 179-180).

Like other workers of color and immigrant workers in the United States, Asian American men and women experience their work world as gendered and as racialized individuals. Economic constraints—and opportunities—have continually restructured relations between Asian American men and women. The existing data show evidence of both greater gender equality and the persistence of male privilege. Even when egalitarianism is enhanced in the home, racial and gender oppression are rampant in the public domain into which Asian American women have moved. Attentive to the intersections of race, gender, and class, this book will explore how a racially and sexually segregated U.S. labor force has restructured the balance of power between Asian American men and women.

Asian Americans and Ideological Racism

In addition to structural discrimination, men and women of color have also been subjected to ideological assaults. According to Stuart Hall (1995), *ideology* refers "to those images, concepts and premises which provide the frameworks through which we represent, interpret, understand, and 'make sense' of some aspect of social existence" (p. 18). The authority to define these "images, concepts, and premises" is a major instrument of power. As Patricia Hill Collins (1990) asserted, a generalized ideology of domination has been essential to the political economy of domination (p. 68). To exercise power, elite white men and their representatives have propagated "controlling images" that brand subordinate groups as alternatively deviant, inferior, or overachieving—and, in so doing, naturalize and normalize sexism, racism, and poverty. For example, it was the myth of the racial inferiority of Mexicans that permitted white Americans to justify the conquest of Mexican territories and the low status of Mexicans in the developing Southwest (Moore & Pachon, 1989, p. 4).

Ideological representations of gender and sexuality are central in the exercise of racial domination. In this racist discourse, the sexuality of men and women of color is constructed to be excessive, animalistic, or exotic in contrast to the "civilized" sexuality of white men and women (Frankenberg, 1993, p. 75). In an analysis of controlling images of African Americans, Collins (1990, p. 68) argued that the constructions of masculinities and femininities along racially differentiated lines provide ideological justification for race, gender, and class oppression. For example, the stereotypic figures of "Jezebel" and "Mammy" have their roots in the sexual abuse and economic exploitation of African American women during slavery and its aftermath. In the same way, in the years immediately following the abolition of slavery, white men constructed the myth of the African American man as sexual aggressor to rationalize the continued oppression and repression of African Americans (Davis, 1981; Frankenberg, 1993, pp. 75-76). These stereotypes effectively exclude black men and women from dominant cultural notions of the masculine and feminine. As Crenshaw (1989, p. 155) observed, "Black men and women live in a society that creates sex-based norms and expectations which racism operates simultaneously to deny."

The ideological assaults on the manhood and womanhood of people of color call attention to the intersections of race and gender: As categories of difference, race and gender relations do not parallel but intersect and confirm each other. As Wiegman (1991) pointed out, "It is the complicity among categories of oppression that enables U.S. culture to enhance hegemonic power" (p. 331). Heeding the interconnections of these systems of inequality, I will historicize and contextualize the ideological representations of Asian American men and women. I will argue that these ideological assaults—the condensations of Asian American men and women's multiple differences into one-dimensional caricatures— construct a reality in which racial, class, and gender oppressions are defensible. Although Asian American women are often portrayed as "hypersexual" and men as "asexual," both stereotypes exist to define and confirm the white man's virility and superiority (Kim, 1990). My goal is to understand how the internalization and renunciation of these stereotypes have (re)shaped sexual and gender politics within Asian America. In particular, I will explore the tensions between Asian American men and women as they balance feminist and nationalist concerns.

Getting There From Here:
Goals, Scope, and Methodology

Throughout their history in the United States, Asian Americans, as immigrants and citizens of color, have faced a variety of economic, political, and ideological assaults that have had direct effects on their gender relations. This book explores how race, class, and gender, as interactive systems, have (re)shaped the rules of gender in the Asian American community. Specifically, it explores how racism, class exploitation, and patriarchy have affected Asian American family relations, labor experiences, and systems of meaning. In this book, *patriarchy* is defined broadly as "the system of male domination and female subordination in economy, society, and culture" (Lim, 1983, p. 76). Though I recognize that patriarchy varies in kind and in degree in different Asian countries, I choose not to detail these differences here. This is so because a comparative analysis of Asian patriarchal systems is beyond the scope of this study. Moreover, I do not wish to essentialize these cultural differences—to present them as if they were unchanging over space and time.

This book is comparative in at least two senses. First, it compares three different historical periods: Chapter 2 examines the implications of the sexually imbalanced communities of pre-World War II Asian America, Chapter 3 explores changes in gender dynamics brought about by World War II and the events of the postwar years, Chapter 4 discusses the increasing heterogeneity of the post-1965 Asian American community and its impact on gender dynamics, and Chapter 5 surveys the changing constructions of Asian American masculinity and femininity over these three historical periods. Second, within each chapter, this book compares and contrasts the experiences of the different Asian American groups, drawing out specificities as well as common patterns. This comparative framework is important given the diversity of the Asian American population along class, ethnic, linguistic, and generational lines. At the same time, because Asian Americans' lives have been and are still strongly influenced by race, it is equally necessary to identify their shared experiences as a racialized people in the United States.

This book is more than a synthesis of existing analyses; it is also a *rereading* of past works to draw out the significance of gender—to identify "invisible" gendered (and racist and classist) structures and processes organizing the worlds of Asian American men and women. This task of assembling and "translating" is necessarily interdisciplinary, moving beyond the confines of sociology to the fields of history, anthropology, literature, critical legal studies, ethnic studies, and cultural studies. It also moves beyond "objective" data to more "subjective" evidence such as autobiographies, biographies, life histories, and literary works. These subjective sources are rich because they "illuminate both the logic of individual courses of action and the effects of system-level constraints within which those courses evolve" (Personal Narratives Group, 1989, p. 6). Moreover, they often expose the rules of male and white domination because "they reveal the reality of a life that defies or contradicts the rules" (p. 7).

Because this book is a rereading of *past works*, it replicates some of the limitations of the field. In particular, it privileges a West Coast paradigm and slights the histories and regions east, west, far north, and south of California (Sumida, 1996). Thus, Chapter 2 begins with the immigration of Chinese laborers to the American West and Hawaii in the 1840s rather than with the much earlier arrival of Filipino sailors in Louisiana in 1793 (Espina, 1988). Though I recognize the "power of place" (Sumida, 1996) and the importance of decentering the West Coast, the goal of this book is not to reconstitute Asian American Studies but rather to (re)read this very history from a gendered perspective. In another critique of the field, Gary Okihiro (1994) has suggested that recentering women in Asian American studies requires a new periodization for Asian American history—one that articulates on the pivot of gender as opposed to race or class relations. Thus, for example, instead of the male-centered periodization scheme of migration and settlement, which focuses on exclusion laws, immigrant laborers, and bachelor communities, a feminist periodization might highlight feminism's rise in Asia and the United States at the turn of the century (p. 91).

Though I agree with Okihiro, the goal of this book is to inject gender into this very "male-centered" history—and, in so doing, to foreground what has been ignored, underrepresented, and misrepresented.

A few words about voice. In the preface to *Black Feminist Thought*, Collins (1990) urged scholars to reconcile subjectivity and objectivity in producing scholarship by using *I, we,* and *our* instead of the more distancing terms *they* and *one* (p. xiv). Though I strongly subscribe to Collins's call for scholars to insert themselves in the text, to be both objective and subjective, I discovered that I was not comfortable using *our* and *we* when discussing the historically specific experiences of the various Asian groups. As a Vietnamese American woman who fled to the United States in 1975 as a refugee, I felt that the specificities of my background did not permit me to use *we* and *our* when writing on the exclusion of Chinese women at the turn of the century, the internment of Japanese Americans during World War II, or the experiences of Filipina nurses in the contemporary period. On the other hand, when discussing the controlling images of Asian Americans (Chapter 5), I felt the need to use *we* and *our* because I understood that outsiders objectify Asian Americans as the "other" by ignoring our specific histories and leveling our differences. That is, regardless of our individualities, Asian Americans continue to be defined as a distinct race and thus need to respond as a group to this racialization (Espiritu, 1992). Thus, the decision to use *I* or *we* or *they* involves more than an individual desire to reconcile the subjectivity and objectivity in our scholarship; it is also necessarily a discursive response to the sociopolitical structures both inside and outside our communities. As a consequence, our political projects always involve the delicate and often frustrating task of balancing the specificities and commonalities of our experiences.

Notes

1. Some notable exceptions are Evelyn Nakano Glenn's *Issei, Nisei, War Bride* (1986), Elaine Kim's *Asian American Literature* (1982), and Nazli Kibria's *Family Tightrope: The Changing Lives of Vietnamese Americans* (1993).

2. The Chinese Exclusion Act of 1882 suspends immigration of laborers for 10 years. The 1917 Immigration Act delineates a "barred zone" from whence no immigrants can come. The 1924 Immigration Act denies entry to virtually all Asians. The 1934 Tydings-McDuffie Act reduces Filipino immigration to 50 persons a year. The 1965 Immigration Law abolishes "national origins" as a basis for allocating immigration quotas to various countries—Asian countries are finally placed on an equal footing.

CHAPTER 2

Stretching Gender, Family, and Community Boundaries, 1840s-1930s

Asians were an indispensable labor force that helped to build the American West and Hawaii.[1] During the second half of the 19th century and the first few decades of the 20th, almost a million people from China, Japan, Korea, the Philippines, and India emigrated to the continental United States and to Hawaii (Chan, 1991a, p. 3). Although these five Asian groups came under different sets of circumstances, all were recruited as workers by U.S. capitalists to meet the need for cheap and manipulable labor in the still-developing U.S. capitalist economy (Chan, 1991a, p. 4). Because what U.S. interests desired was muscle power, they gave little attention to the family and community life of Asian immigrants except as it related to the latter's economic productivity. In most instances, families were seen as a threat to the efficiency and exploitability of the workforce and were actively prohibited. U.S. immigration laws also treated Asian workers as temporary, individual units of labor rather than as members of family groups (Mohanty, 1991, p. 23). During the pre-World War II period, U.S. policies barred the entry of most Asian women. Because men predominated in this period, most research has ignored questions of gender altogether, as if men were without gender. However, a rereading of the historical materials indicates that the shortage of women affected gender relations within Asian America in profound ways: It prevented the formation of patriarchal nuclear families, forced men in womanless households to learn domestic skills, and enhanced the social value of the few women in these immigrant communities (Kim, 1990, p. 74; Dill, 1994, p. 164). In other words, during the pre-World War II era, class exploitation and racist and gendered immigration policies delayed the full transplantation of Asian patriar-

chy in the United States and yielded relatively more social and economic power to the small number of women who were there.

Labor Recruitment, Exclusion Laws, and the Shortage of Women

One of the most noticeable characteristics of pre-World War II Asian
America was a pronounced shortage of women. Some scholars have
attributed the virtual absence of Asian female emigrants, particularly
of Chinese women, to the patriarchal cultural values that restricted the
movement of women in Chinese, Japanese, and Korean societies (Ichioka,
1980; Yung, 1986; Yim, 1989). Other writers have argued that a sojourning mentality, differentials in the cost of living, and hostile conditions
in the American West limited the number of female immigrants (Chan,
1991a, p. 104). There is no question that all or some combinations of
these factors contributed to the low number of Asian female immigrants. But, as I shall argue below, labor recruiting patterns and immigration exclusion policies were the most significant factors in restricting
the immigration of Asian women.

America's capitalist economy wanted Asian male workers but not
their families. To ensure greater profitability from immigrants' labor
and to decrease the costs of reproduction—the expenses of housing,
feeding, clothing, and educating the workers' dependents—employers
often excluded "nonproductive" family members such as women and
children. Detaching the male worker from his household increased
profit margins because it shifted the cost of reproduction from the state
and the employer to the kin group left behind in Asia. Asian women
were also undesirable because of their reproductive powers: They
would bear children who could then claim U.S. citizenship (Lai, 1992,
p. 165). On the Pacific Coast, where a migratory labor force best suited
the growers' needs, the unattached male provided a more flexible
source of labor who could readily be moved to meet short-term labor
needs and expelled when no longer needed (Glenn, 1986, pp. 194-195;
Chan, 1991a, p. 104). A Californian grower told an interviewer in 1930
that he preferred to hire Filipinos because they were without families:
"These Mexicans and Spaniards bring their families with them and I
have to fix up houses; but I can put a hundred Filipinos in that barn
[pointing to a large firetrap]" (quoted in Takaki, 1989, p. 321). Philip
Vera Cruz, a pioneering Filipino laborer, recalled the harsh living
conditions endured by Filipino migrant workers: "The first camp I lived
in had a kitchen that was so full of holes, flies were just coming in and

out at their leisure, along with mosquitoes, roaches, and everything else.
. . . The toilet was an outhouse with the pit so filled-up that it was
impossible to use" (Scharlin & Villanueva, 1992, p. 5). In Hawaii, where
plantation workers remained in one place, plantation managers thought a
feminine presence would have a stabilizing effect on the men. But even
there, the number of women allowed to immigrate was small. For
instance, in the late 1900s, Hawaiian sugar plantation owners specified
that no batch of workers recruited from Japan could contain more than
25% women (Moriyama, 1985, pp. 13-14). Filipinos fared no differently.
A labor commissioner report in Hawaii stated that "plantations have to
view laborers primarily as instruments of production. Their business
interest[s] require cheap, not too intelligent, docile, *unmarried men* [ital-
ics added]" (cited in Sharma, 1984, p. 583).

U.S. immigration policies also permitted more Asian men than
Asian women to enter. Although exclusion laws suspended the immigration of male laborers from China in 1882, from India in 1917, from
Korea and Japan in 1924, and from the Philippines in 1934,[2] U.S. industri-
alists and growers were allowed to bring in replacement workers from
another Asian country. For instance, after the exclusion of Chinese and
Japanese male laborers, U.S. interests mounted an aggressive and well-
organized program to import massive numbers of male workers from
the Philippines (Sharma, 1984). On the other hand, during this same
period, U.S. immigration policies barred the entry of most Asian women.
In fact, a group of Chinese women—prostitutes—were the target of the
very first exclusion act (Chan, 1991b, p. 95). In 1875, Congress passed
the Page Law—named after Congressman Horace F. Page of California—forbidding the entry of Chinese and other "Mongolian" prostitutes,
felons, and contract laborers. In the end, this law reduced the influx of
Chinese women—all of whom immigration officials suspected of being
prostitutes—but not of men because most of the Chinese men who immigrated to North America came on their own and were not contract laborers
per se (Peffer, 1986; Chan, 1991a, p. 3). Only some 1,340 Chinese women
entered the United States between 1875 and 1882, compared with more
than 100,000 men admitted between 1876 and 1882. The proportion of
women among Chinese immigrants decreased from 7.2% in 1870 to a mere
3.6% in 1890 (Okihiro, 1994, p. 64). The 1903, 1907, and 1917 immigration
laws further allowed the deportation of Chinese women suspected of
being prostitutes (Chan, 1991a, pp. 105-106). Given that all Chinese women
were considered prostitutes at that time, "No Chinese woman, regardless
of her social standing, was safe from harassment" (Chan, 1991b, p. 132).

The Page Law, with its focus on defining the *morality* of Asian women as a basis for entry into the United States, illustrates the (het-ero)sexism and racism underlying U.S. immigration laws (Mohanty, 1991, p. 25). In an area of widespread general prostitution, the singling out of Chinese prostitution, ostensibly for moral reasons, exposed a racist concern: the fear that Chinese prostitutes, because of their race, would bring in "especially virulent strains of venereal diseases, intro-duce opium addiction, and entice young white boys to a life of sin" (Chan, 1991b, p. 138). The depiction of the sexuality of Asian women as immoral and different from that of white women served to underline the depravity of the "Orientals" and became yet another reason for advocating the exclusion of Asians (Mazumdar, 1989, pp. 3-4).

Transformed into a more general restriction on Chinese female immigration, the antiprostitute clause of the Page Law "contributed to the process that made Chinese families forbidden institutions in a land that did not want them" (Peffer, 1986, p. 44). Without these immigration restrictions, the numbers of Chinese women immigrants might have been considerably larger. As it was, by 1882, the sex ratio in Chinese immigrant communities was already sharply skewed. The nadir was reached in 1890, 15 years after the enactment of the Page Law, when the sex ratio stood at a high 27 to 1 (Chan, 1991a, p. 106). Thus a conjugal family life for most Chinese immigrant men did not exist until at least after the third decade of the 20th century (Lyman, 1968, p. 323). As Alfred Wang (1988) observed, "No other racial groups have been sub-jected to worse *legalized* . . . sexual deprivation than the Chinese male immigrants between 1868 . . . and 1952" (p. 18). The barring of women, brought about by class interests, racism, and (hetero)sexism, led to the desexualization of Asian men. As Donald Goellnicht (1992) suggested, the targeted exclusion of Chinese women was a "deliberate agenda" by mainstream culture "to prevent any increase in the Chinese American population and to undermine the virility of Chinese and Chinese Ameri-can men" (pp. 194-195).

In 1882, responding to anti-Chinese agitation and to the economic downturns of the 1870s, Congress enacted the Chinese Exclusion Law, which suspended the entry of Chinese laborers for 10 years but ex-empted merchants, students and teachers, diplomats, and travelers from its provisions (Chan, 1991a, p. 54). Chinese exclusion was ex-tended in 1892 and again in 1902 and was made indefinite in 1904. Because these laws contained no specific clauses on women, the courts, in general, ruled that the legal status of Chinese females paralleled that of their husbands. Thus, because the 1882 exclusion law suspended the immigration of laborers, their wives were similarly denied entry. Similarly, merchants' wives were allowed to enter because their husbands were among the "exempted classes." These rulings conformed to a racist and (hetero)sexist ideology of a patriarchal nuclear family in that Asian women were not "accorded subject status but [were] always assumed to be legal appendages of men" (Mohanty, 1991, p. 26). Until the rescission of the exclusion laws in 1943, women constituted only about 12% of Chinese immigration, and most of them came as wives of merchants or of U.S. citizens (Yung, 1990, p. 70). The class bias of the exclusion laws meant that Chinese laborers, who constituted the majority of the Chinese immigrants, could not establish conjugal families in the United States. It also suggested that within the general racial antagonism against Chinese, "There emerged differential degrees of discrimination according to class" (Chan, 1991b, p. 138).

Japanese immigrants, who began arriving soon after the passage of the 1882 Chinese Exclusion Law, also faced exclusion. But whereas Chinese exclusion was imposed quickly and suddenly, the U.S. government—out of deference to the national sensibilities of Japan, a rising military power in the Pacific Basin—restricted Japanese immigration in stages, thereby allowing Japanese men more time to send for wives. The 1907 Gentlemen's Agreement terminated all labor immigration from Japan but allowed the entry of wives and children of Japanese residents in the United States. Taking advantage of this window of opportunity between 1900 and 1920, many men summoned wives from Japan. The influx of women from Japan during these two decades allowed the Japanese immigrant communities to establish more resident families than their Chinese counterparts. In 1900, of the 850 Japanese women among 18,000 men in the three Pacific Coast states (a sex ratio of 21 to 1), about 400 were married. Ten years later, the number of women had increased to over 8,000, with almost 5,600 married, reducing the sex ratio to 6.5 to 1. By 1920, there were more than 22,000 married women among a total Japanese female population of 38,000 on the mainland (Ichioka, 1988, p. 164; Chan, 1991a, pp. 107-108). Because few bachelors could afford to return to Japan to seek brides, many resorted to the "picture bride" practice—arranged marriages facilitated by the exchange of photographs. The majority of wives who entered Japanese immigrant society between 1910 and 1920 came as picture brides (Ichioka, 1988, p. 165). Anti-Japanese groups soon agitated against the alleged fertility of Japanese women and demanded a stop to the influx of picture brides. In 1920, the Japanese government acquiesced to U.S. public opinion by denying passports to picture brides. Finally, the Immigration Act of 1924 stopped Japanese immigration entirely by barring the entry of "aliens ineligible to citizenship." In this way, the 1924 act nullified the Gentlemen's Agreement and denied admission even to wives of U.S. citizens (Ichioka, 1988).

Even fewer Filipino, Korean, and Indian women immigrated to the United States. According to Lasker (1969), of the estimated 102,069 Filipinos who arrived in Hawaii from 1907 to 1929, 87% were males (Lasker, 1969). On the mainland, almost all Filipino immigrants were prime-age single male workers. Out of every hundred Filipinos who migrated to California during the 1920s, 93 were males, 80 of whom were between 16 and 30 years of age (Wallovitts, 1972, p. 21). Among the approximately 7,000 Koreans who came to Hawaii between 1902 and 1905, only 10% were women[3] (Yu, 1987). The female population among Korean communities increased somewhat between 1910 and 1924 with the arrival of more than 1,000 picture brides. They came with Japanese passports issued to them as colonial subjects of Japan under the terms of the Gentlemen's Agreement (Takaki, 1989, p. 56). Fewer than a dozen Asian Indian women immigrated to the United States before World War II.[4] Of the 474 Indians who arrived in the United States in 1909, none were women (Chan, 1991a, p. 109; Okihiro, 1994, p. 67).

Stretching the Boundaries of Family

Like other people of color, Asians in the United States have had to struggle to maintain their family and community life in a context that is not supportive of and is often actively hostile to their institutions (Glenn, 1983, p. 371). The labor recruitment practices coupled with the restrictive and exclusionary laws instituted by the dominant white culture prevented family formation or re-formation by Asian immigrants. In an analysis of the exclusion of Chinese women, Megume Dick Osumi (1982) pointed out that the anti-Chinese movement prevented the procreation of a second generation of Chinese, "thereby insuring that the 'Chinese problem' would eventually disappear" (p. 8). In the face of these assaults to family units, Asian immigrants struggled to create and maintain some semblance of family life, often by redefining and extending the concept of "family."

Bachelor Societies

Unable to send for wives and legally prohibited from marrying white women, most Asian laborers were lonely bachelors or absentee husbands, destined for a harsh life without families. Trapped in a womanless world, these men had to rearrange their reproductive tasks. Thus, their food and shelter might come in the form of a boardinghouse, their social life in a local bar, and their female companion in a bordello. Bereft of family life, many men idled away their leisure time in gambling dens, pool halls, bar-restaurants, or brothels. A Japanese immigrant woman recalled that "many of the Issei [first-generation immigrants] indulged in gambling. It took care of their spare time" (Kikumura, 1981, p. 28). In San Francisco, nearly all the Chinese laborers lived on the streets on Sundays simply because they had "nothing to do, and no-where else to go" (quoted in Takaki, 1989, p. 127). "Life didn't mean too much to us," recalled a Chinese laborer bitterly (Nee & Nee, 1973, p. 24). Unlike the Chinese and Japanese, Filipinos did not engage extensively in ethnic enterprises. In 1933, at the height of Filipino immigration to the Pacific West Coast, only one Filipino grocery store was found in Los Angeles. Twenty-three years later, there were only six.[5] Because Filipinos did not develop their own ethnic sections in cities, Filipino farm laborers usually congregated in Chinatowns on weekends, where "there were many happenings . . . dances, prostitution, whatever." For many of them, the pool hall was "their world" (cited in Takaki, 1989, p. 337).

The skewed sex ratio enhanced the social value of Asian immigrant women and gave them more options in their dealings with men. Given their small numbers, single women were highly prized as sexual and marital partners. For instance, the few *Pinays* (Filipinas) already in the United States commanded attention from the single *Pinoys* (Filipinos). "Back in the 1920s," recalled Terry Rosal, "there weren't that many Filipinas. One Pinay to one hundred Pinoys. And regardless of the shape or the age of the Pinay, she was a queen." Similarly, Belen de Guzman Braganza had no trouble getting dates in Seattle: "I could date anyone. You could count [the number of Filipina] women in your two hands" (quoted in Takaki, 1989, p. 340). Even married women had to fend off unwanted male attention. According to a Japanese woman who came to the United States with her husband in 1923, "Everywhere we worked there were few married couples and the rest were single men. Those who had wives bragged. Consequently, the women without any children had many men pursuing them. . . . Many times men approached me and said, 'Let me do it with you and I'll give you money' " (Kikumura, 1981, p. 30). Prostitutes also found themselves in demand as potential wives. For example, the San Francisco-based Presbyterian Mission Home for Chinese women prostitutes, which operated from 1874 until 1939, received marriage inquiries from Chinese immigrant men from all over the country. These mission marriages raised the social status of these former prostitutes, who otherwise would have been destined for lives of prostitution, neglect, abuse, or hardworking poverty (Pascoe, 1990). The positive consequences of these mission marriages for prostitutes offer one of the many examples of the contradictions that arise in Asian American history.

Surrounded by bachelors eager to marry, an Asian immigrant woman dissatisfied with her husband and her marriage had more alternatives than her sisters in Asia. Anecdotal evidence indicates that the skewed sex ratio allowed women to take actions to free themselves from unwanted marriages. In the Korean immigrant community in Hawaii, adultery was frequent enough to warrant a system of fines for first and *subsequent* "offenses." Runaway wives were also common (Kim, 1990, pp. 74-75). In retaliation, Korean and Japanese men used their fraternal associations to institutionalize patriarchal control of "their" women (Srole, 1987, p. 5). Prewar Japanese immigrant presses regularly printed *kakeochi* notices—public notices submitted by husbands searching for their runaway wives—as a means of social control. Branded as "adulteresses" or "immoral hussies," these women were ostracized and eventually forced to leave the immigrant community. The Japanese associations also acted as the "moral watchdogs" of Japanese communities. As a matter of policy, all Japanese associations refused to have any dealings with absconding couples. Given the network of associations, absconding couples had to resettle in a place where there were no Japanese to elude social ostracism. In 1916, the rate of desertion was sufficiently high that the Japanese American Association of America deliberated on the problem at its annual meeting. The desertion problem prompted the association to issue a "Guide to the United States" for new arrivals, instructing these women on how to conduct themselves aboard ship, how to manage a household, and how to behave in American society (Ichioka, 1988, pp. 169-172).

Although beset with social problems, Asian bachelor communities sustained lonely men with conviviality, warmth, and some semblance of family life. With few women, children, and older people around, young male immigrants often redefined and stretched the boundaries of "family" to include nonkin. Chinese and Japanese immigrants formed a complex network of kinlike organizations with co-ethnics to perform the crucial functions traditionally carried out by extended families, clans, or lineages (Lyman, 1974; Ichioka, 1977; Lai, 1987). Punjabi migratory workers also formed substitute families with individuals who shared the same religion, language, social background, and values. For mutual aid, companionship, and security, these workers traveled together in gangs from farm to farm. According to Bruce La Brack (1982), when a gang member died, the others paid for the funeral expenses, sent photographs of the body to India, and contributed money to the widow of the deceased.

In terms of their own cultural values, enforced childlessness stripped Asian men of their manhood and condemned them to a life of "perpetual boyhood" in their own communities (Kim, 1990, p. 74). According to Chinese culture, "Among the three unfilial acts, not having offspring is the worst" (Wang, 1988, p. 24). Missing the company of wives and small children, single Asian men adopted and were adopted by the few families that were around. In the Filipino community in Hawaii, as many as 200 men would be invited to be godparents at every religious ceremony, from baptism to marriage. This modified *compadre* system incorporated fictive relatives into the kinship network and enabled many single men to affiliate themselves with a family system (Agbayani-Siewert & Revilla, 1995). Connie Tirona, one of the few Filipino children around in northern California in the 1930s, became the "adopted daughter" of many of the bachelor friends of her parents. These *manongs*[6] bought Tirona her first bicycle and purchased pageant tickets from her "by the fistful." Tirona recalled the joy that her family's visits brought to these lonely *manongs* who labored in the Sacramento-San Joaquin area:

> [Our family] went to see them almost every week or every other week.
> . . . It was so beautiful there when we visited them. . . . The *manongs*
> would fix up their rooms immaculately. . . . After eating they would
> play guitars and mandolins, and we, as little children of the families,
> would sing and dance. . . . They were so happy. I especially remember
> when we sang the Visayan songs. You could see the tears on the faces
> of these grown men. (Espiritu, 1995, p. 69)

Similarly, California-born Jean Park related that Korean bachelors from nearby towns often visited her family in Taft. One of the bachelors, Mr. Kim, became an uncle to Jean and her siblings. Whenever Mr. Kim visited her family, he would play with the children, driving them everywhere and treating them to ice cream, soda, and candy (Takaki, 1989, p. 288). Tirona's and Park's favored status as "adopted daughters" indicates that in a community where families were few, daughters were often prized. Although the traditional preference for sons might have remained strong, the scarcity of children, and of women in general, raised the status of daughters within the family and community (Kim, 1990, p. 74). Moreover, the second-generation daughters were in high demand as prospective brides. These young women were often married off to much older bachelors who had postponed marriage until they had saved enough money to afford a family. As these women became more independent, however, they insisted on selecting their own husbands. Judy Yung (1986) reported that even before the 1920s, second-generation Chinese American women sought refuge in missionary homes or eloped to avoid arranged marriages (p. 49).

Immigrant Families

The existence of bachelor societies did not mean that the majority of male emigrants were single: A good number married shortly before they went abroad but left their wives behind (Chan, 1991a, p. 104). In 1900, although 38% of Chinese males over the age of 15 were married, there was only 1 Chinese female to every 26 Chinese males in the United States (Coolidge, 1909/1968, p. 19). Similarly, although a 1909 Immigration Commission survey of 474 male "Hindoo" farmworkers found that 215 were married, all 215 of the wives had remained in India (Leonard, 1982, p. 67). As Okihiro (1994) reminded us, "Asian men in America were not solitary figures moving in splendid isolation but were intimately connected to women in Asia who built and maintained the solid world of family and community" (p. 68).

The split household is not unique to Asians. The history of other immigrant groups indicates that most men leave their wives behind in the first phase of their settlement in a new land. Where the Asian pattern deviates from the norm is that due to the legal exclusion of Asian women, the split-household arrangement lasted much longer than that of other immigrant groups—in some cases, for several generations (Glenn, 1983, p. 39). Despite the difficulties faced by split households, the majority of these families remained intact, and some eventually reunited—sometimes after generations (see Chapter 3 of this book). These transnational families survived partly because they pursued coordinated economic activities, with the husband in the United States specializing in income-producing activities and the wife and other relatives in the home village carrying out the functions of reproduction, socialization, and the rest of consumption (Glenn, 1983). The existence of these split households reminds us that national borders do not always constitute social borders (Yanagisako, 1995, p. 291).

Given the predominance of men in pre-World War II Asian America, sociological and historical studies of this period have focused principally on men—their experiences as bachelors and laborers in the United States (Nee & Nee, 1973; Lyman, 1974). There is comparatively little information on the "intricate and dynamic pattern of relations" between male-dominated communities and women-headed households in the home villages in Asia or on the women themselves (Okihiro, 1994, p. 68). The spotty information on the lives of the wives who stayed behind suggests that the split-household arrangement was both liberating and oppressive: It gave some women more independence but saddled most with a disproportionate share of household reproductive tasks as well as a life without the company and assistance of their husbands.

As income producers, migrant men controlled the greater share of income and were less accountable to their families while in the United States than were the women who stayed behind (see Hondagneu-Sotelo, 1994). Chinese migrant husbands often sent remittances directly to their kin—and not to their wives—to ensure that the wives would "remain chaste and subject to [the husbands'] ultimate control" (Glenn, 1983, p. 39). Virtual widows, these wives were expected to serve their husbands' parents and remain sexually faithful while their distant husbands were free to visit prostitutes or take on other wives (Okihiro, 1994, p. 74). The following Toishan folk song captures the anguish of these "married widows":

> I am still young, with a husband, yet a widow.
>
> The pillow is cold, so frightening.
>
> Thoughts swirl inside my mind, chaotic like hemp fibers;
>
> Separated by thousands of miles, how can I reach him?
>
> Thinking of him tenderly—
>
> I toss and turn, to no avail.
>
> He is far away, at the edge of the sky by the clouds;
>
> I long for his return, especially since it's midnight now.
>
> (Hom, 1983, p. 129)

The anguish became unbearable for some. Moola Singh, who migrated to America from the Punjab in 1911, intended to send for his wife once he had saved enough money for her fare. But she died before he could return. "She good, nice looking, healthy, but she love," explained Singh. "You know love, person no eat, worry, then maybe die" (quoted in Takaki, 1989, p. 309). But other wives did not remain faithful. Asahiki Sawada sailed to San Francisco in 1904, promising his wife that he would return a wealthy man. After 6 years of hard work, Sawada sent for his wife, only to learn that she had divorced him and remarried in the interim (Nakano, 1990, p. 29).

Unlike Asahiki Sawada, most migrant husbands did not earn enough money to return home a rich man or to send for their wives. The prolonged absence of men increased the burden but also the authority of women who stayed behind. As Ruth Hsiao (1992) suggested, Chinese wives "take on domineering aspects as the husbands' self-esteem diminishes" (pp. 153-154). Similarly, Linda Ching Sledge (1980) noted that after the emigration of male villagers to distant lands, Cantonese women assumed total family governance and subsequently developed a strong tradition of womanly self-sufficiency and aggressiveness. This tradition persisted among the few Cantonese women who were allowed to join their husbands in the United States during the more than six decades of exclusion (pp. 9-10).

The split-household arrangement, enforced and maintained by racist and gendered U.S. immigration policies, made possible the maximum exploitation of male workers. Because the cost of reproduction was borne largely by the kin group in Asia, the labor of male workers could be bought relatively cheaply (Glenn, 1983, p. 39). The women who stayed behind also played a crucial role in producing the next generation of workers for overseas capitalists. Many of the Asia-born children, especially the grown sons, became the next generation of immigrant workers when they came to the United States to join their fathers. Stanford Lyman (1968) reported that many of the China-born sons were brought to the United States to help out and eventually take over their fathers' businesses (pp. 328-329).

As stated earlier, of all the Asian groups, the Japanese, and to a lesser extent the Koreans, under the terms specified in the Gentlemen's Agreement, had the most opportunity to summon their wives and reconstitute their families in the United States. That these women were willing to travel to the United States to marry unknown men suggests that they were independent, adventurous, and ambitious. For many women, becoming a picture bride was viewed as an opportunity to travel and to circumvent the social restrictions on women in their home countries. As one Korean woman who came to the United States as a picture bride exclaimed,

> Ah, marriage! Then I could get to America! That land of freedom with streets paved of gold! . . . Since I became ten, I've been forbidden to step outside our gates, like all the rest of the girls of my day. . . . Becoming a picture bride, whatever that was, would be my answer and release. (Sunoo & Sunoo, 1976, p. 149)

Although detailed studies of picture brides have not been made, scattered sources suggest that many of the picture brides from Korea had received some sort of modern education, with some having attended high school and a few even receiving college education. They were the by-products of the modern movement that took place in Korea at the turn of the century. Most picture brides had also worked outside the home as teachers and nurses. Even the less educated picture brides had regularly attended church and Bible classes (Yang, 1987, p. 172).

Arriving in the United States with high hopes, most of the picture brides were shocked and disappointed to find older and unattractive men waiting for them on the deck. Pyong Gap Min (1995) reported that the mean age difference between Korean husbands and wives was 14 years (p. 202). Woo Hong Pong Yun described her reaction on sighting her husband in Honolulu who turned out to be 13 years her senior: "When I see him, he skinny and black. I no like. No look like picture. But no can go home" (quoted in Takaki, 1989, p. 72). A few disappointed picture brides refused to join their husbands and asked to be sent back to Japan (Ichioka, 1988, p. 167). The men also were disillusioned with their photo brides. Some bridegrooms claimed that their wives did not physically correspond with their photographs and rejected them practically at dockside. Others claimed that their wives were too "high toned" or were not fit for the rigors of pioneer life (Nakano, 1990, p. 29). Despite these initial objections, many of these arranged marriages endured—partly due to the lack of alternatives.

Work and Changing Gender Relations

The gender-stratified and racially hierarchical labor market in the United States effectively relegates people of color, women, and most especially women of color to the lowest-status and lowest-paying jobs in society. From 1850 to World War II, Asian men and women provided cheap and exploitable sources of migrant labor to meet the needs of a rapidly developing U.S. industrialized economy (Bonacich & Cheng, 1984). U.S. race relations also changed dramatically in the late 19th century. The end of slavery ushered in a new set of segregation laws demarcating the place of people of color in society. These new racial restrictions, along with the rising conflict between capital and labor during U.S. industrialization, severely circumscribed the labor market opportunities of these early Asian immigrants (Mar & Kim, 1994, p. 14).

Racial discrimination separates the labor experience of Asian immigrants from that of Europeans. During this period, white men were considered "free labor" and could work in the growing metallurgical, chemical, and electrical industries, while Asian men were racialized as "coolie labor" and confined to nonunionized, dead-end jobs in the agricultural and service sectors (Chan, 1991a, chap. 2). Asian immigrants were particularly vulnerable because they were not allowed to become naturalized citizens. Their alien status transformed them into tractable labor and increased the ability of capital to discipline and exploit them—an example of the collusion of racism and class interests (Bonacich, 1984, pp. 165-166). From the turn of the century until the 1929 Depression, although jobs were plentiful in San Francisco, Chinese men still occupied the lowest tier as laborers, servants, factory workers, laundrymen, and small merchants. According to Light (1972), "Prior to 1940, discrimination in employment virtually eliminated opportunities for Chinese in the general labor market" (p. 8). Later-arriving Asian groups likewise found themselves in the least desirable sectors of the labor market (Chan, 1991a, chap. 2). Until the Great Depression, the majority of Filipinos, about 60%, toiled in the fields as unskilled migrant laborers. In 1925, Filipinos constituted over 80% of the asparagus labor force, numbering approximately 7,000. Because of the long hours of stooping, extreme heat, and dust involved, cutting asparagus is the most difficult job a farmworker can do, with even experienced, able-bodied laborers passing out from heat prostration and exhaustion (Espiritu, 1995, p. 10).

Like Asian men, most Asian women labored in agricultural and service sectors as farm women, prostitutes, cooks, laundresses, and seamstresses (Chan, 1991a, pp. 109-110). Given the lack of decent-paying jobs for Asian American men, women's labor was important to economic subsistence. In this sense, the arrival of Asian women ensured the physical survival of Asian America not only because of their reproductive powers but also because of their productive powers. In Hawaii, for example, the commissioner of labor report noted in 1901 that whereas most other wives "engaged solely in home duties," most Japanese wives worked outside the home. These women often received the lowest pay of any group. Japanese female field hands, for example, received an average wage of only 55 cents per day in 1915, compared to the 78 cents paid to Japanese male field hands (Takaki, 1989, p. 135). Though minimal, their income was nevertheless critical for the family finances due to the low wages paid to Japanese men. Gail Nomura (1989) estimated that the earnings of the Japanese wife, on the average, added a significant 35% to the family income (p. 140). Even merchants' wives contributed to the household income by taking in sewing and fancy embroidery (Chan, 1991a, p. 109). This situation is not unique to Asian Americans. In an overview of immigrant women, Morokvasic (1984) reported that the labor of immigrant women has been one of the few ways for immigrant men to accumulate capital (p. 891).

The small number of U.S.-born Asians, most of whom came of age during the 1920s, also did not fare well in the labor market. Although these men and women were English speaking, highly educated, and Western oriented, most could not find jobs commensurate with their education and training (Chan, 1991a, p. 113). The Great Depression certainly decreased the economic opportunities available to second-generation Asian Americans. But racial discrimination played a crucial role in segregating the workforce. According to Judy Yung (1986), during this period, white women were able to find employment in clerical work, social work, nursing, and teaching, but Chinese American women could find jobs only as elevator girls, stock girls, "Oriental" hostesses, and housemaids. Even those few women with advanced degrees in medicine, education, and social work could not find work outside Chinatown. Katie Moy, the first Chinese and only woman to graduate from the College of Pharmacy of Detroit in 1925, recalled that "whenever I applied for a job, I was turned down because I was Chinese and a girl" (quoted in Yung, 1986, p. 57).

Below, I review three types of work performed by Asian men and women during the pre-World War II period: prostitution, domestic service, and self-employment. This is not meant to be an exhaustive review of the labor experiences of Asian Americans during this period. Instead, I chose these three cases because they seem to illustrate best the contradictions and opportunities presented to Asian men and women in this era. In each case, I explore the impact that these contradictions and opportunities had on gender relations.

Prostitution

Living in a world of men, Asian laborers sought a sexual outlet and intimacy from prostitutes. Lyman (1968) reported that at the end of the 19th century, the Chinatowns of America's cities "were honeycombed with brothels" (p. 326). Most Chinese male sojourners viewed prostitutes as providers of a necessary service to their largely bachelor community (Tong, 1994, p. 123). In this sense, prostitutes assisted in the capitalist exploitation of migrant men insofar as they helped to perpetuate the labor system of unattached male workers (Cheng, 1984).

Chinese and Japanese prostitutes were among the pioneers of their respective immigrant societies. Their migration was sometimes prompted by a desire for freedom, but for the most part, it was induced and orchestrated by men for their profit and exploitation. Whereas the majority of white prostitutes came as independent professionals or worked in brothels for wages, Chinese and Japanese prostitutes were almost always lured, tricked, or forced into prostitution by men (Yung, 1986, p. 18; Ichioka, 1988). In 1870, census takers counted 2,794 Chinese female workers; 77% declared themselves as prostitutes and the rest as service-related workers. A decade later, partly as a result of the antiprostitute clause in the 1875 Page Law, only 44% of the 1,726 Chinese women workers were engaged in prostitution (Tong, 1994, p. 30). Japanese prostitutes began to appear in the late 1800s and increased in the 1890s. In 1900, the majority of the 985 Japanese female immigrants were prostitutes (Ichioka, 1988, pp. 28-29). But in time, with the arrival of picture brides, Japanese prostitutes were vastly outnumbered by wives (Chan, 1991a, p. 107). In contrast to the Chinese but more similar to the Japanese, Korean male emigrants had little trouble bringing in wives through the picture bride practice; consequently, relatively fewer Korean women entered as prostitutes (Tong, 1994, p. 169).

In a community of womanless men, control over the provision of sex provided those who had it with wealth and power (Nakano, 1990, p. 24). Yung (1986) listed the many groups that profited from the prostitution trade: the procurers and importers who brought women to the United States; the brothel owners who controlled the labor of the prostitutes; the high-binders, policemen, and immigration officials who were paid to protect the business; and the white Chinatown property owners who charged these brothels exorbitant rents (p. 18). Prostitutes were especially profitable for their owners. "At an average of 38 cents per customer and seven customers per day," Hirata (1979) calculated, a lower-grade prostitute would earn about 850 dollars per year and 3,404 dollars after four years of servitude. Since women in the inferior dens were kept at the subsistence level, the cost of maintaining them must not have exceeded 8 dollars per month or 96 dollars per year per person. (p. 234)

Hirata concluded that "these calculations indicate that the owner would begin to make a profit from the prostitute's labor in the first year of service!" (p. 234).

Initially, individual women entrepreneurs controlled the lucrative business of prostitution in Chinese quarters. Ah Toy, who arrived alone in San Francisco in 1849 from Hong Kong to "better herself," became the earliest and most successful Chinese courtesan in San Francisco. Within a year of her arrival, Ah Toy became an independent courtesan of means, owning a brothel of Chinese women on Pike Street (now Waverly Place). Men reportedly lined up a block long and paid an ounce of gold ($16) just "to gaze upon the countenance of the charming Ah Toy" (Gentry, 1964, p. 52). Ah Toy was also a popular figure in the courtroom, where she appeared numerous times to defend her trade and to sue those clients who had paid her with brass fillings instead of gold (Yung, 1986, p. 4). But rival secret societies soon wrestled the control of prostitution out of the hands of women (Lyman, 1968; Cheng, 1984). Prostitution was so lucrative that rival tongs often fought for its control. Violent tong wars in the 1870s and 1880s often began with disputes over possession of a Chinese prostitute (Yung, 1986, p. 18).

As laborers, prostitutes were exploited as cheap workers. Not all earned wages; many simply worked for their owners, who retained all of their earnings and exploited them further in manual labor as seamstresses, cooks, and washerwomen (Okihiro, 1994). Pimps or brothel owners—the center of male authority and power in the establishment—sometimes used force to coerce reluctant new prostitutes to perform and to compel all women to work harder and bring in more money. An unknown number of Chinese prostitutes were physically abused by their owners—and their customers. On the other hand, the value that owners and customers placed on prostitutes' services allowed these women to retain some control over their own lives "even as they gave their oppressors the illusion of total submission" (Tong, 1994, p. 145). For example, prostitutes retaliated against their oppressors by stealing, restricting the sexual activities that took place, and running away (Tong, 1994).

In sum, the skewed sex ratio of Chinese and Japanese immigrant communities provided an opportunity for these immigrants, if they so desired, to profit from prostitution. Although some women profited, many more men derived their fortunes from the labor of women prostitutes. These men then "inscribed their names and deeds in histories that slighted and marginalized the selfsame women who had been instrumental in their rise to power" (Okihiro, 1994, pp. 78-79). The history of prostitution in pre-World War II Asian America suggests that although immigration provided some benefits for women, it provided men many more opportunities to control and exploit them.

Domestic Service

Feminist scholars have argued accurately that domestic service involves a three-way relationship between privileged white men, privileged white women, and poor women of color (Romero, 1992). The material experiences of Asian Americans during the pre-World War II period (particularly the shortage of women) suggested at least two other forms of racial and gender subjugation of domestic workers: one involving Asian men and women and the other involving Asian men and white men and women. In the first instance, women earned money by providing domestic services—cooking, washing, ironing, and sewing—for the many unattached men in their communities. In her life story, *Quiet Odyssey: A Pioneer Korean Woman in America,* Mary Paik Lee related that while her father labored in Riverside's citrus groves, her mother contributed to the family income by cooking for some 30 single men who worked with her father, making their breakfast at 5 a.m., packing their lunches, and serving them supper at 7 p.m. (Lee, 1990). Although domestic work provided women with much-needed income, it also buttressed male privilege by perpetuating the concept of reproductive labor as women's work. This gender subordination was particularly oppressive for married women who had to perform domestic duties for the bachelors as well as for their own families. As Chan (1991a) pointed out, "In the evening hours, while men relaxed, women continued to work at various chores" (p. 109).

The racialized and gendered immigration policies and labor conditions discussed earlier also forced Asian men into "feminized jobs" such as domestic service, laundry work, and food preparation. Due to their noncitizen status, the closed labor market, and the shortage of women, Asian immigrant men, first Chinese and later Japanese, substituted to some extent for female labor in the American West. David Katzman (1978) noted the peculiarities of the domestic labor situation in the West in this period: "In 1880, California and Washington were the only states in which a majority of domestic servants were men" (p. 55).

At the turn of the century, lacking other job alternatives, many Chinese men entered into domestic service in private homes, hotels, and rooming houses (Daniels, 1988, p. 74). Whites rarely objected to Chinese in domestic service. In fact, through the 1900s, the Chinese houseboy was the symbol of upper-class status in San Francisco (Glenn, 1986, p. 106). As late as 1920, close to 50% of the Chinese in the United States still worked as domestic servants (Light, 1972, p. 7). Large numbers of Chinese also became laundrymen, not because laundering was a traditional male occupation in China but because there were very few women of any ethnic origin—and thus few washerwomen—in gold-rush California (Chan, 1991a, pp. 33-34). Chinese laundrymen thus provided commercial services that replaced women's unpaid labor in the home. White customers were prepared to patronize a Chinese laundryman because as such he "occupied a status which was in accordance with the social definition of the place in the economic hierarchy suitable for a member of an 'inferior race'" (cited in Siu, 1987, p. 21). In her autobiographical fiction *China Men*, Maxine Hong Kingston presented her father and his partners as engaged for long periods each day in their laundry business—a business considered so low and debased that in their songs, they associate it with the washing of menstrual blood (Goellnicht, 1992, p. 198). A Chinese laundryman described his harsh life: "I am not an old man yet, but I feel old. How can a man feel good when he is forced into an occupation he doesn't like. But I get used to it. After you are at it for so many years, you have no more feeling but to stay on with it" (quoted in Wong, 1976, p. 339). The existence of the Chinese houseboy and launderer—and their forced "bachelor" status—further bolstered the stereotype of the feminized and asexual or homosexual Asian man. Their feminization, in turn, confirmed their assignment to the sector of the state's labor force that performed "women's work."

Japanese men followed Chinese men into domestic service. By the end of the first decade of the 20th century, the U.S. Immigration Commission estimated that 12,000 to 15,000 Japanese in the western United States earned a living in domestic service (Chan, 1991a, pp. 39-40). Many Japanese men considered housework beneath them because in Japan only lower-class women worked as domestic servants (Ichioka,

1988, p. 24). Studies of Issei occupational histories indicate that a domestic job was the first occupation for many of the new arrivals; but unlike Chinese domestic workers, most Issei eventually moved on to agricultural or city trades (Glenn, 1986, p. 108). Filipino and Korean boys and men also relied on domestic service for their livelihood (Chan, 1991a, p. 40). In his autobiography *East Goes West*, Korean immigrant writer Younghill Kang (1937) related that he worked as a domestic servant for a white family who treated him "like a cat or a dog" (p. 66).

Filipinos, as stewards in the U.S. Navy, also performed domestic duties for white U.S. naval officers. During the 94 years of U.S. military presence in the Philippines, U.S. bases served as recruiting stations for the U.S. armed forces, particularly the navy. Soon after the United States acquired the Philippines from Spain in 1898, its navy began actively recruiting Filipinos—but only as stewards and mess attendants. Barred from admissions to other ratings, Filipino enlistees performed the work of domestics, preparing and serving the officers' meals and caring for the officers' galley, wardroom, and living spaces. Ashore, their duties ranged from ordinary housework to food services at the U.S. Naval Academy hall. Unofficially, Filipino stewards also were ordered to perform menial chores such as walking the officers' dogs and acting as personal servants for the officers' wives (Espiritu, 1995, p. 16).

As domestic servants, Asian men became subordinates of not only privileged white men but also privileged white women. The following testimony from a Japanese house servant captures this unequal relationship:

> Immediately the ma'am demanded me to scrub the floor. I took one hour to finish. Then I had to wash windows. That was very difficult job for me. Three windows for another hour! . . . The ma'am taught me how to cook. . . . I was sitting on the kitchen chair and thinking what a change of life it was. The ma'am came into the kitchen and was so furious! It was such a hard work for me to wash up all dishes, pans, glasses, etc., after dinner. When I went into the dining room to put all silvers on sideboard, I saw the reflection of myself on the looking glass. In a white coat and apron! I could not control my feelings. The tears so freely flowed out from my eyes, and I buried my face with my both arms. (quoted in Ichioka, 1988, pp. 25-26)

The experiences of Asian male domestic service workers demonstrate that not all men benefit equally from patriarchy. Depending on their race and class, men experience gender differently. Although male domination of women may tie all men together, men share unequally in the fruits of this domination. For Asian American male domestic workers, economic and social discrimination locked them into an unequal relationship with not only privileged white men but also privileged white women (Kim, 1990, p. 74).

The racist and classist devaluation of Asian men had gender implications. The available evidence indicates that immigrant men reasserted their lost patriarchal power in racist America by denigrating a weaker group: Asian women. In *China Men,* Kingston's immigrant father, having been forced into "feminine" subject positions, lapses into silence, breaking the silence only to utter curses against women (Goellnicht, 1992, pp. 200-201). Kingston (1980) traced her father's abuse of Chinese women back to his feeling of emasculation in America: "We knew that it was to feed us you had to endure demons and physical labor" (p. 13). Asian men also oppressed Asian women by denying them any joy in life. In Hisaye Yamamoto's short story "Seventeen Syllables," the Issei wife inserts beauty and meaning into her life of endless toil by writing poetry at night. Unable to tolerate his wife's independence, the Issei husband forbids his wife to write poetry. In a crucial scene, the husband loses his temper and burns the poetry prize that she has won for her haiku. Broken, the woman turns to her daughter and issues a stern warning: " 'Rosie,' she said urgently, 'Promise me you will never marry!' " (Kim, 1982, pp. 59).

On the other hand, some men brought home the domestic skills they learned on the jobs. Anamaria Labao Cabato related that her Filipino-born father, who spent 28 years in the navy as a steward, is "one of the best cooks around" (Espiritu, 1995, p. 143). Leo Sicat, a retired U.S. Navy man, similarly reported that "we learned how to cook in the Navy, and we brought it home. The Filipino women are very fortunate because the husband does the cooking. In our household, I do the cooking, and my wife does the washing" (Espiritu, 1995, p. 108). Further (as will be discussed in Chapter 3), in some instances, the domestic skills that men were forced to learn in their wives' absence were put to use when husbands and wives reunited in the United States. The history of Asian male domestic workers suggests that the denigration of women is only one response to the stripping of male privilege. Another is to institute a revised domestic division of labor and gender relations in the family.

Self-Employment

Excluded from employment in the industrial and trade labor market by racial discrimination and white working-class hostility, many Asian immigrants became shopkeepers, merchants, and small businessmen. In 1929, Asian immigrants, principally Chinese and Japanese, "owned one-and-a-half times as many businesses per 1,000 population as other residents of the United States" (Myrdal, 1944, p. 310). The Chinese ethnic economy was based on retail businesses, service, vice, and entertainment. "Wherever the Chinese are," observed Rose Hum Lee in 1942,

> it has been possible to count the variations in the way they can earn their living on the fingers of the hand—chop suey and chow mein restaurants, Chinese art and gift shops, native grocery stores that sell foodstuffs imported from China to the local Chinese community and Chinese laundries. (cited in Takaki, 1989, p. 251)

In some instances, the domestic skills that men learned in the absence of women were put to good use in certain businesses such as laundries, small food stores, and restaurants. Similarly, according to a 1909 survey of 2,277 Japanese businesses conducted by the Immigration Commission, the Japanese ethnic economy was based primarily on retail and service (Ichihashi, 1932, p. 110). Unlike the Japanese and Chinese, Filipinos, Koreans, and Asian Indians did not engage extensively in ethnic enterprise (Takaki, 1989, pp. 270, 307, 336).

The labor of Asian women was indispensable to the establishment and success of these family enterprises. In Hawaii, Asian immigrant men with wives were more able than single men to move away from plantation wage labor into small family-operated businesses. Chan (1991a) reported that Asian women did everything possible to move their families away from plantation work as soon as possible (p. 110). They took in laundry, grew vegetables, and undertook whatever additional work they could to help save up enough money to open their own small businesses. Many took these initiatives in an attempt to secure a better future for their children. On the Pacific Coast, Asian immigrant women worked as unpaid labor in various small family enterprises, playing a critical role in establishing the economic base of Asian American communities (Kim, 1990, p. 74). These small businesses were profitable principally because they took advantage of the unpaid labor of family members—women and children included (Glenn, 1986, pp. 11-12). Beside running the household and raising the children, many Chinese immigrant women "spent every other waking hour" helping their husbands operate laundries, restaurants, and stores. While the husband ran the business in front, the woman performed much of the manual labor in back, such as ironing and folding customers' laundry, preparing food and washing dishes in restaurant kitchens, or stocking merchandise in stores. Wong Loy, who came to the United States in 1927, spent 15 to 16 hours a day ironing in her husband's laundry with a baby strapped to her back. "I worked so hard that my body was sore all over and I had to have *kim sha* [a Chinese folk remedy] every two weeks to draw out the soreness" (quoted in Yung, 1986, p. 43). Their lives of endless toil left no time for socializing and few opportunities for learning English and assimilating into U.S. society. In the 38 years that Yee Shee Lee worked in the family laundry, she left it only three times—all to attend family association celebrations in a nearby city (Yung, 1986, p. 44).

The unpaid labor of Japanese immigrant women was especially critical in enabling Issei males to exit the unskilled wage labor market and to form a thriving ethnic enclave economy. As they left the railroads, mines, and lumber mills, many Japanese immigrants entered agricultural employment. By 1909, 6,000 Japanese had become farmers (Ichihashi, 1932, pp. 162-163). As they entered farming, many Japanese men sent for their wives or picture brides—not only for their companionship but also for their labor (Takaki, 1989, p. 190). The formation of Japanese families in the United States provided the Issei farmer with the free labor force needed to operate an independent truck farm. The availability of unpaid household labor allowed Issei truck farmers to compete effectively with white farmers and subsequently to gain a dominant share of the produce market. Together, Issei men and women converted marginal, dusty, and desert lands into lush and profitable agricultural fields and orchards (Takaki, 1989, p. 191). By 1910, Japanese were leaving wage labor rapidly and establishing ethnic enterprises in both rural and urban areas (Nee & Wong, 1985, p. 295).

Korean picture brides, most of whom were better educated than men, also helped their husbands move ahead. Highly motivated, these women were active in economic ventures. Their small numbers, their education, and their economic contributions all worked in tandem to create an opportunity in which Korean men as well as women could transform traditional patriarchy. Eui-Young Yu (1987) reported that apparently "women in the early Korean community enjoyed better status and position than women in contemporary society" (p. 185). But more often than not, traditional patriarchy persisted in these family enterprises in that most women had to work a double shift—in the home and in the family business. Japanese wives complained about their husbands' refusal to help with the housework: "We worked from morning till night, blackened by the sun. My husband . . . didn't even glance at the house work or child care. No matter how busy I was, he would never change a diaper" (Ito, 1973, p. 251). Kimiko Ono described her "double day":

> I got up before dawn with my husband and picked tomatoes in the greenhouse. At around 6:30 a.m. I prepared breakfast, awakened the children, and all the family sat down at the breakfast table together. Then my husband took the tomatoes to Pike Market. I watered the plants in the greenhouses, taking the children along with me. . . . My husband came back at about 7 p.m. and I worked with him for a while, then we had dinner and put the children to bed. Then I sorted tomatoes which I had picked in the morning and put them into boxes. When I was finally through with the boxing, it was midnight—if I finished early—or 1:30 a.m. if I did not. (Ito, 1973, p. 251)

Patriarchy also surfaced when men insisted that they were the business owners and their wives the helpers, even though women's contributions were often equal to or greater than men's. John Gee, a son of a Chinese laundryman, described the unequal gender division of labor in his and other family laundry businesses:

> Sometimes actually the women do more than the men, but I don't think—I don't like to say this—but in some cases like my dad's, he figures he owns the business and that he's the boss. And sometimes the men have the habit of being a little lax at working, and they expect you to do a little bit more. (Wong, 1976, p. 343)

Asian male entrepreneurs also exploited Asian women as paid laborers. Joe Shoong, the owner of National Dollar Stores and one of the richest Chinese businessmen in the United States in the 1930s, relied heavily on the exploitation of the labor of Chinese women: The women's dresses sold in the National Dollar Stores were sewn by low-paid Chinese garment workers employed in San Francisco's Chinatown. In 1937, these women organized themselves into the Chinese Ladies Garment Workers Unions and struck against the garment factory owned by the National Dollar Store. Their strike lasted 13 weeks, the longest in Chinatown's history, but the workers lost in the end when the employer closed the factory rather than conceding to their demands (Takaki, 1989, p. 252).

Conclusion

The material existences of Asian American men and women during the pre-World War II period contradicted the traditional constructions of "man" and "woman." During this period, racist and gendered immigration policies and labor conditions emasculated Asian men, forcing them into "bachelor" communities and into "feminized" jobs that had gone unfilled due to the shortage of women. In the same fashion, women who stayed behind in Asia were denied access to a "normative family," while those in the United States worked outside the home, often performing heavy "men's work" in the farms and on the plantations. The (re)construction of gender in prewar Asian America emerged from this sociohistorical context. The racial patriarchy of U.S. society limited Asian men's social power vis-à-vis the larger society and thus delayed the full transplantation of Asian patriarchy in the United States. Although women were still exploited economically and socially by Asian men, their small numbers and their economic contributions offered unusual opportunities for them, as marriage partners and as income producers, to raise their social status. These gender patterns would shift once again as the United States went to war with Japan in the mid-1940s and as more women were allowed to join their husbands in the United States during the postwar years.

Notes

1. Hawaii was an independent kingdom from 1810 to 1893, a republic between 1894 and 1900, and a territory of the United States from 1900 to 1959.

2. For a history of the exclusion of Asian immigrants, see Chan (1991a, chap. 3).

3. Korean emigration to Hawaii and to the United States lasted only two and a half years, from December 1902 to May 1905. In 1902, representatives of the Hawaiian Sugar Planters' Association (HSPA) brought Korean workers to the islands to counter the growing militance of Japanese plantation workers. In 1905, when Japan declared Korea a "protectorate," the Japanese government prohibited Korean emigration to Hawaii to protect Japanese plantation workers in Hawaii and to stamp out overseas Korean independence activities. Consequently Korean immigration to the United States was much smaller than that of the Chinese and Japanese. Between 1902 and 1905, approximately 7,000 Korean adults emigrated, nearly 10% of whom were women (Takaki, 1989, pp. 53-57; Chan, 1991a, pp. 15-16).

4. The period of Indian immigration was extremely short. Canada was the preferred destination for many Indians. But when Canada began placing restrictions on Indian immigration in 1908, Indians started coming

directly to the United States. The peak years of Indian immigration into the United States were from 1907 to 1910. In 1917, Congress passed the 1917 Immigration Law, which delineated an "Asiatic barred zone" from which no immigrants could come. This law effectively prohibited immigration from India. Altogether, only 6,400 Asian Indians came to the United States during this period (Takaki, 1989, pp. 62-65; Chan, 1991a, pp. 18-23).

5. Ronald Takaki (1989) summarized several reasons for the notable lack of Filipino merchants in the United States. Since Spanish colonial days, retail needs in the Philippines had been serviced by Chinese merchants. Consequently few of the indigenous people acquired experience in trade. Moreover, by the time Filipinos came to the United States, the Chinese and Japanese had already established a foothold in the retail trade and preempted the entry of Filipino retailers. Finally, the low participation of Filipinos in business activity reflected the transiency of the migrants. Most Filipinos were single male migratory workers shuttling back and forth along the Pacific Coast, moving constantly with the harvests of specialty crops (pp. 336-337).

6. *Manong* literally means "uncle," a term of respect used for old-timers.

CHAPTER 3

Changing Lives

World War II and the Postwar Years

World War II marked an important turning point in the history of Asians in the United States. During the war years, Japanese America was ripped apart as more than 100,000 persons of Japanese ancestry were relocated in concentration camps. The wartime internment devastated the lives of all internees but permanently eroded the Issei (first-generation) men's economic position and weakened their patriarchal authority over the family. The lives of Chinese, Koreans, Filipinos, and Asian Indians, in contrast, improved because their ancestral nations were allies of the United States. The wartime services of these men did a great deal to reduce white prejudice against Asians, earned many U.S. citizenship, and helped to rescind exclusion laws, thus renewing immigration from Asia. In particular, the War Brides Act of 1945, which allowed Asian wives and children of U.S. servicemen to enter as non-quota immigrants, brought large numbers of Asian immigrant women to the United States. Their arrival revitalized family life but also wreaked havoc in these male-dominated and resource-starved communities. The longtime bachelors were unable to meet the material needs of their newly (re)established families and were ill prepared for the day-to-day relationships with their wives. Finally, the wartime labor shortage and postwar economic prosperity generated unprecedented occupational opportunities not only for U.S.-born Asian men but also for many U.S.-born Asian women. These social and economic changes pushed more Asian Americans into contact with the larger U.S. society, accorded more economic independence to U.S.-born Asians, and frag-

AUTHOR'S NOTE: The poem by Nikaido Gensui appeared in "Footprints: Poetry of the American Relocation Experience," in *Amerasia Journal, 3,* pp. 115-117, and is used with permission.

mented Asian America more clearly than in the past along class lines. All these changes challenged the traditional patriarchal structure as many young men and women were freed for the first time from the confinement of the previously closed ethnic communities.

Changing Power Relations:
The Wartime Internment of Japanese Americans

Birds
Living in a cage,
The human spirit.

Nikaido Gensui
(1976, p. 116)

Immediately after the bombing of Pearl Harbor, the incarceration of Japanese Americans began. On the night of December 7, 1941, the Federal Bureau of Investigation (FBI) began taking into custody persons of Japanese ancestry who had connections to the Japanese government. Working on the principle of guilt by association, the security agencies simply rounded up most of the Issei leaders of the Japanese community. Initially, the federal government differentiated between alien and citizen Japanese Americans, but this distinction gradually disappeared. On February 19, 1942, President Franklin Delano Roosevelt signed Executive Order 9066, arbitrarily suspending civil rights of U.S. citizens by authorizing the "evacuation" of 120,000 persons of Japanese ancestry into concentration camps, of whom approximately 50% were women and 60% were U.S.-born citizens (Matsumoto, 1989, p. 116). It was during this period that the Japanese American community discovered that the legal distinction between citizen and alien was not nearly so important as the distinction between white and yellow (Daniels, 1988, chap. 6). Years later, in a speech in support of redress and reparations, Congressman Robert Matsui (1987), who had been an infant in 1942, asked in anguish, "How could I as a 6-month-old child born in this country be declared by my own government to be an enemy alien?" (p. 7584). Calling attention to the construction of Asian Americans as the "foreigner-within," Lisa Lowe (1966) has argued that Americans of Asian descent, even as citizens, remain the symbolic "alien"—the metonym for Asia who by definition cannot share in the American nation.

The camp environment, with its lack of privacy, regimented routines, and new power hierarchy, inflicted serious and lasting wounds on Japanese American family life. In the crammed 20-by-25-foot "apartment" units, tensions were high as men, women, and children struggled to re-create family life under very trying conditions. The disappearance of the traditional family meal also increased the distance between parent and child. In the camps, the internees ate mass-prepared meals in large mess halls, and children often preferred to sit with their friends at separate tables from their parents (Kitagawa, 1967, p. 84). A former Nisei (second-generation immigrant) internee recounted the havoc that mess hall living wreaked on her extended family:

> Before Manzanar,[1] mealtime had always been the center of our family scene. In camp, and afterward, I would often recall with deep yearning the old round wooden table in our dining room in Ocean Park . . . , large enough to seat twelve or thirteen of us at once. . . . Now, in the mess halls, after a few weeks had passed, we stopped eating as a family. Mama tried to hold us together for a while, but it was hopeless. Granny was too feeble to walk across the block three times a day, especially during heavy weather, so May brought food to her in the barracks. My older brothers and sisters, meanwhile, began eating with their friends, or eating somewhere blocks away, in the hope of finding better food. (Houston & Houston, 1973, pp. 30-31)

The internment also transformed the balance of power in families: Husbands lost some of their power over wives, as did parents over children. Until the internment, the Issei man had been the undisputed authority over his wife and children: He had been both the breadwinner and the decision maker for the entire family. Now "he had no rights, no home, no control over his own life" (Houston & Houston, 1973, p. 62). Most important, the internment reversed the economic roles, and thus the status and authority, of family members. With their means of livelihood cut off indefinitely, Issei men lost their role as breadwinners. Despondent over the loss of almost everything they had worked so hard to acquire, many Issei men felt useless and frustrated, particularly as their wives and children became less dependent on them. Daisuke Kitagawa (1967) reported that in the Tule Lake relocation center, "The [Issei] men looked as if they had suddenly aged ten years. They lost the capacity to plan for their own futures, let alone those of their sons and daughters" (p. 91).

Issei men responded to this emasculation in various ways. By the end of 3 years' internment, formerly enterprising, energetic Issei men had become immobilized with feelings of despair, hopelessness, and insecurity. Charles Kikuchi remembered his father, who "used to be a perfect terror and dictator," spending all day lying on his cot: "He probably realizes that he no longer controls the family group and rarely exerts himself so that there is little family conflict as far as he is concerned" (Modell, 1973, p. 62). But others, like Jeanne Wakatsuki Houston's father, reasserted their patriarchal power by abusing their wives and children. Stripped of his roles as the protector and provider for his family, Houston's father "kept pursuing oblivion through drink, he kept abusing Mama, and there seemed to be no way out of it for anyone. You couldn't even run" (Houston & Houston, 1973, p. 61). The experiences of the Issei men underscore the intersections of racism and sexism, showing how men of color live in a society that creates sex-based norms and expectations (e.g., man as breadwinner) that racism operates simultaneously to deny (Crenshaw, 1989, p. 155).

Whereas camp life eroded the status and authority of the Issei men, it provided comparative benefit to Issei women. As discussed in Chapter 2, ever since their arrival in the United States, most Issei women had endured lives of continuous drudgery: They had reared children, kept house, and toiled alongside their husbands in labor-intensive jobs. For these women, life in the camps was a "highly deserved holiday" (Kitagawa, 1967, p. 89). The communally prepared meals and minimal living quarters (with no running water or cooking facilities) freed Issei wives from most domestic responsibilities and enabled them to attend to themselves (Kim, 1990, pp. 73-74). A good number of women filled their newfound spare time with adult classes, hobbies, religious meetings, cultural programs, and visits with friends—all activities previously prohibited because of their long workdays both inside and outside the home (Matsumoto, 1989, pp. 116-117). Daisuke Kitagawa (1967) recorded the changing lives of Issei women in the Tule Lake relocation center:

> For the first time in their lives, they had something akin to free time in a substantial amount, and in many different ways they blossomed out. Most of them took employment of some kind with the work corps . . . , [but] the work was not too hard; moreover, they had the companionship of women from a similar situation and like background. Once the day's work was done, the rest of the time was completely at their disposal. . . . Issei women unwittingly became the happiest people in the relocation center. They even began to look younger. (pp. 89-90)

This is not to say that Issei women enjoyed their internment years, but only that their lives improved relative to those of the Issei men. Also, as much as Issei women relished their newfound independence, they also missed their position as "queen of the household." Deprived of their homes, the traditional site of the construction of their womanhood, some Issei women fought to regain their household authority. Charles Kikuchi recalled that his mother

> will do anything to retain her place in the family and won't be pushed aside. Even at meals she has her methods. Since she doesn't do the cooking, she attempts to maintain her position by carrying all the plates home and by dividing the desserts or watching our [younger siblings] unnecessarily. (Modell, 1973, p. 140)

Camp life also widened the distance and deepened the conflict between the Issei and their U.S.-born children. At the root of these tensions were growing cultural rifts between the generations as well as a decline in the power and authority of the Issei fathers. The cultural rifts not only reflected a general process of acculturation but were accelerated by the degradation of everything Japanese and the simultaneous promotion of Americanization in the camps (Chan, 1991a, p. 128; see also Okihiro, 1991, pp. 229-232). The younger Nisei also spent much more time away from their parents' supervision. With no competition from white students, the Nisei snatched the leadership positions in the schools: They became class presidents, yearbook editors, pom-pom girls, athletic heroes, and social "ins" (Kim, 1982, pp. 162-163; Kitano, 1991a, p. 155). Enamored with their newfound social positions, the Nisei spent most of their "waking hours without either seeing or being seen by their parents" (Kitagawa, 1967, p. 86). According to a former Nisei internee, "Once the weather warmed up, it was an out-of-doors life, where you only went 'home' at night, when you finally had to: 10,000 people on an endless promenade inside the square mile of barbed wire that was the wall around our city" (Houston & Houston, 1973, p. 35). In such a setting, Issei parents lost their ability to discipline their children, whom they seldom saw during the day. Much to the chagrin of their conservative parents, young men and women began to spend more time with each other unchaperoned at sports events, dances, and other school functions. According to Charles Kikuchi, camp life broke down some of the parents' protectiveness over their daughters: "Many of the parents who would never let their daughters go to dances before do not object so strenuously now" because they realized that their children could not "stay home night after night doing nothing without some sort of recreational release" (Modell, 1973, pp. 81-82). Freed from some of the parental constraints, the Nisei women socialized more with their peers and also expected to choose their own husbands and to marry for "love"—a departure from the old customs of arranged marriage (Matsumoto, 1989, p. 117). Once this occurred, the prominent role that fathers played in marriage arrangements—and by extension in their children's lives—declined (Okihiro, 1991, p. 231).

Privileging U.S. citizenship and U.S. education, War Relocation Authority (WRA) policies regarding camp life further reversed the power hierarchy between the Japan-born Issei and their U.S.-born children. In the camps, only Nisei were eligible to vote and to hold office in the community council; Issei were excluded because of their alien status. Daisuke Kitagawa (1967) recorded the impact of this policy on parental authority: "In the eyes of young children, their parents were definitely inferior to their grown-up brothers and sisters, who as U.S. citizens could elect and be elected members of the Community Council. For all these reasons many youngsters lost confidence in, and respect for, their parents" (p. 88). Similarly, the WRA salary scales were based on English-speaking ability and on citizenship status. As a result, the Nisei youths and young adults could earn relatively higher wages than their fathers. This shift in earning abilities eroded the economic basis for parental authority (Matsumoto, 1989, p. 116). College-educated Nisei who had been trained as doctors, dentists, or teachers found work in their professions for the first time behind barbed wire. These Nisei professionals were at the top of the (albeit low) pay scale, earning $19 dollars per month. Other workers were paid $16 dollars for skilled work and $12 dollars for unskilled or menial work (Kitagawa, 1967, p. 80).

Though no mass evacuation of Japanese took place in Hawaii,[2] the territory's martial law plans—applied to all of Hawaii's residents but contrived specifically to contain the Japanese—also reversed the roles of parent and child. In a study of the anti-Japanese movement in Hawaii, historian Gary Okihiro (1991) detailed this military-induced social inversion:

> The status of *issei* fell as the standing of *nisei* rose with the differential treatment given the generations by the military. *Issei* bore the stigma of enemy alien; *nisei* were tainted, but nevertheless wooed and cajoled toward Anglo conformity. *Issei* spoke the language of the enemy; *nisei* translated government orders, radio and print news, and social cues, intonations, and sanctions for parents who did not know English well. *Issei* represented an obsolete mentality, an Old World flavor that had become distasteful. *Nisei* symbolized the future, a new direction and style, in full pursuit of the American dream. (p. 231)

A young Nisei woman in Hawaii praised this transition: "Like a symbol of medieval restraint, the kimono has been almost forsaken, and women have been freed of the stiff obi bindings and wrappings" (cited in Okihiro, 1991, p. 231). Okihiro argued that this reversal of roles contributed to social disruption in the Japanese community, which was "a goal of the strategy for defense because it weakened the will and ability to resist" (p. 229).

Women's work experiences also changed in complex ways during the internment years. In one of the many ironies that the internment produced, Nisei women found more job opportunities in the relocation camps than they did on the outside. Organized as model cities, each camp offered a wide array of jobs for these young women, ranging from clerical work in the administration offices, medical care in the hospitals, and busing tables in the mess halls to serving as assistant teachers in the makeshift classrooms or as writers and artists for the camp newspapers. Although many Nisei women had worked before the war, the relative parity in wages in the camps altered family dynamics and accorded them relatively more status in the family (Matsumoto, 1989, pp. 116-117; Nakano, 1990, pp. 150-151).

The student relocation programs further removed Nisei men and women from the patriarchal constraints of their families. In 1942, concerned educators organized the nongovernmental National Japanese American Student Relocation Council (NJASRC) to enable Nisei college students to complete their education. NJASRC persuaded colleges and universities outside the restricted western defense zone to accept Nisei students, facilitated the admissions of these students, and secured their leave clearances. In the years 1942 to 1946, NJASRC placed 4,084 Nisei students in colleges. Of the first 400 students to leave camps, a third were women. Matsumoto (1989) attributed the women's desire to relocate to their increasing sense of independence and self-confidence developed in the camps. A Nisei woman recounted her determination to leave: "Mother and father do not want me to go out. However, I want to go so very much that sometimes I feel I'd go even if they disowned me. What shall I do? I realize the hard living conditions outside but I think I can take it" (quoted in Matsumoto, 1989, p. 118). In yet another relaxation of patriarchal control, Issei parents, despite their initial reservations, gradually sanctioned their daughters' departures for education and employment in the Midwest and East. A postwar study of a group of 1,000 relocated students found that 40% were women. Many Nisei women gravitated to the field of nursing; by July 1944, there were more than 300 Nisei women in over 100 nursing programs in 24 states (Matsumoto, 1989, pp. 118-120).

At war's end in August 1945, Japanese Americans had lost much of the economic ground that they had gained in more than a generation. The majority of Issei women and men no longer had their farms, businesses, and financial savings; those who still owned property found their homes dilapidated and vandalized and their personal belongings stolen or destroyed (Broom & Riemer, 1949). The internment also ended Japanese Americans' concentration in agriculture and small businesses. In their absence, other groups had taken over these ethnic niches. This loss further eroded the economic basis of parental authority because Issei men no longer had businesses to hand down to their Nisei sons (Broom & Riemer, 1949, p. 31). Historian Roger Daniels (1988) declared that by the end of World War II, "The generational struggle was over: the day of the Issei had passed" (p. 286). Issei men, now in their 60s, no longer had the vigor to start over from scratch. Forced to find employment quickly after the war, many Issei couples who had owned small businesses before the war returned to the forms of manual labor in which they had begun a generation ago. Most men found work as janitors, gardeners, kitchen helpers, and handymen; their wives toiled as domestic servants, garment workers, and cannery workers (Yanagisako, 1987, p. 92). An Issei woman likened the effort to find the first job out of camp to "a race" (Glenn, 1986, pp. 79-83). As the Issei strove to eke out a living, their children struggled to join mainstream postwar United States—with varying degrees of success.

Improved Lives:
Chinese, Korean, Filipino, and Indian Americans

While the lives of Japanese Americans were being ripped apart, the lot of persons of Chinese, Korean, Filipino, and Asian Indian ancestry improved because their ancestral nations were allies of the United States. The start of World War II dramatically changed American public attitudes toward these groups, particularly toward Filipinos and Chinese (Feria, 1946-1947; Chan, 1991a, p. 121). The military exploits of Filipino soldiers, both in the Philippines and in the United States, did a great deal to reduce white prejudice against Filipino Americans. When the United States declared war against Japan in December 1941, President Franklin D. Roosevelt incorporated the Philippine armed forces into the United States Armed Forces in the Far East (USAFFE). Fighting alongside American soldiers in defending Bataan and Corregidor during the spring of 1942, the heroism and courage of Filipino troops were widely publicized in newsreels and newspaper headlines across the United States. Meanwhile, large numbers of Filipinos in the United States were inducted into the armed forces. Their status as U.S. nationals forgotten, many became citizens through mass naturalization ceremonies held before induction. A. B. Santos, a Filipino immigrant who came to the United States in the 1920s, recounted his experience with the draft and subsequent naturalization:

> When World War II came, I got drafted into the U.S. Army. They drafted me in 1943 even though I was a foreigner, a noncitizen. . . . On Saturday morning, I reported to Los Angeles. When I got there, they swore me in as a U.S. citizen. I did not even have to file an application. So that was how I became a U.S. citizen. (Espiritu, 1995, p. 42)

Because most Filipinos were males of draft age, some 16,000 were called up under the first draft in 1942 (Espiritu, 1995, p. 17).

Sizable numbers of Chinese also joined and served in the U.S. armed forces. According to a New York City survey, almost 40% of the Chinese population were drafted, the highest draft rate of any ethnic group. Historian Peter Kwong (1979) noted the historical origin of this high draft rate: "Because of the Exclusion Act, most Chinese had no dependents and according to the law were the first called" (pp. 114-115). Thomas Chinn (1989) estimated that between 15,000 and 20,000 Chinese men and women served in all branches of the U.S. military (pp. 147-150). Previously maligned as the "heathen Chinee," and "mice-eaters," the Chinese were characterized in a 1942 Gallup poll as "hardworking, honest, brave, religious, intelligent, and practical" (Chan, 1991a, p. 121). Harold Liu of New York's Chinatown expounded on the improved images of Chinese in the United States:

> In the 1940s for the first time Chinese were accepted by Americans as being friends because at that time, Chinese and Americans were fighting against the Japanese and the Germans and the Nazis. Therefore, all of a sudden, we became part of the American dream. . . . It was just a whole different era and in the community we began to feel very good about ourselves. . . . My own brother went into the service. We were so proud that they were in uniform. (cited in Takaki, 1989, p. 373)

In late 1943, as a gesture of goodwill toward China and of U.S. commitment to democracy, Congress rescinded all Chinese exclusion laws, granted Chinese immigrants the right of naturalization, and provided for the admission of 105 Chinese each year. In 1946, the Luce-Celler bill conferred similar naturalization rights and a small immigration quota of 100 to Asian Indians and Filipinos. In contrast, Japanese and Koreans did not receive these same rights until 1952 (Chan, 1991a, p. 122). As discussed below, these new rights renewed immigration from Asia and transformed forever the family and community life of Asians in the United States.

Eligibility for naturalization, coupled with President Roosevelt's 1941 Executive Order prohibiting racial discrimination in employment, also spearheaded the socioeconomic advancement of the Asian American population. As citizens, qualified Asians were able to secure professional licenses and subsequently to participate in all those economic activities hitherto denied to them as "aliens ineligible for citizenship" (Wong, 1980, p. 520). The right of naturalization also came at a fortuitous time—when defense industries were experiencing an extraordinary boom and were desperately short of human resources. The acute labor shortage; the confinement of the Japanese in relocation camps, creating a sudden vacuum; and the improvement in public images of (non-Japanese) Asians all created employment opportunities for Asians. As the country's industrial base expanded, many Filipino men found jobs in factories, trades, and wholesale and retail sales. Sociologist R. T. Feria (1946-1947) reported that in southern California, the shipyards of Wilmington and San Pedro and the plants of Lockheed, Douglas, and Vultee clamored for Filipino labor. Chinese Americans likewise entered the shipyards and aircraft factories as engineers, technicians, workers, and clerks. Finally able to break away from the Chinatown economy, thousands of laundrymen and waiters rushed to the higher-paying industrial jobs. In Los Angeles, some 300 Chinese laundry workers left their shops to work on the construction of the ship *China Victory*. In 1943, Chinese constituted approximately 15% of the shipyard labor force in the San Francisco Bay Area. They also seized the high-paying jobs in the defense industries at the Seattle-Tacoma Shipbuilding Corporation, the shipyards of Delaware and Mississippi, and the airplane factories on Long Island (Wong, 1980, pp. 511-512; Takaki, 1989, p. 374).

Although there exist no detailed statistics on the wartime employment of Asian Americans, fluctuations between the 1940 and the 1950 censuses provide a rough indication of changes in their occupational status. According to Ling-chi Wang's analysis of census data, in 1940 only about 1,000 Chinese held professional and technical jobs among

36,000 gainfully employed. Ten years later, some 3,500 did so among 48,000 workers. The majority of these were Chinese male professionals who worked as engineers and technicians in war industries. The war also opened up employment opportunities for Chinese women: The number of women in the labor force increased from 2,800 in 1940 to 8,300 in 1950 (Chan, 1991a, p. 122).[3] The majority of these women worked as office clerks in defense industries; the number of Chinese female clerical workers increased from 750 in 1940 to 3,200 in 1950. But others also worked as mechanics and as professionals in private companies. In 1940, 200 Chinese women held professional or technical jobs; in 1950, over 1,150 did (Yung, 1986, p. 67; Chan, 1991a, p. 122).

In sum, World War II changed the economic fortunes of Asians in the United States by opening employment in labor-starved defense industries. This wartime employment opportunity helped many Asian men and women to break down race-based and gender-based occupational barriers and to launch new careers outside their ethnic communities not only during but also after the war (Yung, 1986, p. 67; Chan, 1991a, p. 122).

Asian Americans and Postwar America: The Emerging Middle Class

The 15 years after World War II marked a period of largely positive change for Asian Americans. By the end of World War II, the U.S. economy had emerged as the preeminent urban industrial economy, generating numerous high-paying semiskilled jobs in the manufacturing sector. Other postwar conditions—the infrastructure development, the housing boom, the increasing U.S. military role around the world, and the expanding role of both the local and federal governments—likewise produced a wealth of high-wage jobs. As is usual during economic boom periods, race relations improved considerably during the postwar years. Legal restrictions based on race were removed due to the relatively affluent times and the growing civil rights movement. As a result of these changes in race relations and the strength of the U.S. economy, significant numbers of U.S.-born Asians—the children of the 1910s and 1920s—became increasingly middle class (Daniels, 1988, chap. 7; Mar & Kim, 1994, pp. 19-20).

As detailed below, Japanese and Chinese Americans, particularly the women, benefited from the postwar expanding economic opportunities. Although the postwar period was marked by the increasing labor force participation of all U.S. women, Chinese and Japanese women entered the labor force in even greater numbers. By 1960, 47% of Japanese American women and 42% of Chinese American women were in the labor force, as compared with 34% of all U.S. women. In contrast, because few Filipina women immigrated prior to the war, there was not a significant number of American-born Filipino workers entering the postwar labor market. Although some immigrant Filipino workers left farm work as a result of the economic expansion, most remained in low-paying service or manufacturing jobs (Mar & Kim, 1994, p. 23).

The postwar years marked a turning point for Japanese Americans in the labor force. The wartime destruction of their family businesses coupled with the postwar economic expansion moved Japanese Americans away from a community-based economy to one that depended on employment in the general economy (Mar & Kim, 1994). As Japan became America's "junior partner" in containing communism in eastern Asia, the U.S. public perception of Japanese Americans grew correspondingly more favorable. With the lessening of overt discrimination, more Nisei men and women were finally able to use their U.S. education to enter the mainstream labor market—in engineering, medical, sales, and clerical occupations—and to make steady and uninterrupted economic progress. As indicated above, the postwar years registered a sharp increase in the number of Japanese American women in the labor force. This increase reflects not only expanded job opportunities but also women's desire to help their families recover the internment losses and the movement of Issei and Nisei women out of unpaid family labor (due in large part to the losses of family businesses) and into the general labor force. Whereas Nisei men still encountered discrimination in white-collar work, Nisei women workers were in high demand to fill clerical and civil service positions. Though some—primarily Issei women—still toiled as domestics and garment workers, the majority of second-generation women worked as typists, stenographers, and office clerks (Matsumoto, 1989, pp. 121-122; Nakano, 1990, p. 189; Nishi, 1995, p. 122). By 1970, well over half of all working Nisei women were in white-collar professional, managerial, sales, or clerical positions (Glenn, 1986, pp. 83-89).

Though the second-generation Chinese Americans also moved away from the traditional prewar occupations, they did so at a slower pace than the Japanese Americans. The greater survival of Chinese ethnic enterprises meant the continuation of employment in low-paying restaurant and garment work, particularly for the aging old-timers and the impoverished immigrants arriving in the 1950s (see below). At the same time, substantial numbers of American-born men and women landed professional and technical jobs, again concentrating in engineering and medical fields (Mar & Kim, 1994, p. 23). Though their progress was temporarily halted during the "Cold War," when Communist China became the despised enemy, Chinese Americans managed to survive and steadily prospered (Chan, 1991a, pp. 141-142).

In sum, compared to the pre-World War II period, the postwar years brought unprecedented economic and social progress for Asian American women and men. U.S.-born Asians, particularly Chinese and Japanese, were able for the first time to find employment in the growing professional and technical occupations. But we must not overemphasize the extent of this progress. The tide did turn; Asian Americans did benefit. On the other hand, many Asian Americans continued to be denied access to high-paying craft, manufacturing, and construction jobs (Mar & Kim, 1994, p. 23). Another recurrent problem was discrimination in earnings. According to a 1965 report published by the California Trade Employment Practices Commission, for every $51 earned by a white male Californian, Japanese males earned $43 and Chinese males $38—even though Chinese and Japanese men did become slightly better educated than the white majority. No corresponding figures were reported for women (Daniels, 1988, p. 315). Finally, well-qualified Japanese and Chinese Americans continued to be passed over for promotions to administrative and supervisory positions (Kitano & Daniels, 1988, p. 47).

New Arrivals:
The "Separated" Wives, War Brides, and Refugees

Unlike previous immigration flows, Asian immigration during the postwar period (1946-1965) was overwhelmingly female (Chan, 1991a, p. 140). The partial liberalization of immigration policies permitted many "split households" to be reunited and encouraged many single Asian men to rush "home" to find wives (Kitano, 1991b, p. 199; Wong, 1995, p. 65). Of great importance to the Asian American community—particularly to the Chinese American community—was the 1946 act permitting Asian spouses of U.S. citizens to skirt restrictive immigration quotas by entering as "nonquota immigrants" (Lee, 1956, p. 14). Another important piece of immigration legislation was the War Brides Act of 1945. Amended in 1947 to include veterans of Asian ancestry, this act gave many Asian GIs a 3-year window of opportunity to marry in Asia and to bring their brides back to the United States, where they started families. Together, these immigration policies brought an unprecedented number of Asian women—mostly "separated" wives and war brides—to the United States and in so doing changed forever the previously male-dominated bachelor societies (Lee, 1956; Hsiao, 1992, p. 153).

Between 1945 and 1953, over 12,000 Chinese immigrants entered the United States, of whom 89% were female (Lee, 1956, p. 15). This female dominance continued through the 1950s, when women constituted from 50% to 90% of the Chinese entries during particular years (Chan, 1991a, p. 140). Among this wave of immigrant women were older wives who had been separated from their Chinese American husbands for as many as 15 years. The end of the war and changes in immigration policies finally allowed them to join their husbands in the United States (Lee, 1956, p. 14). Despite their nonquota immigration status, these women, at the point of entry, were still harassed, detained, and threatened with deportation. In 1948, 41-year-old Wong Loy attempted to jump from the 14th floor of an immigration building when told that she would be deported. That same year, 32-year-old Leong Bick Ha hanged herself from a shower pipe after having been detained for 3 months and performing poorly at her interrogation. In protest, 100 Chinese women detainees went on a hunger strike. Confronted with such adverse publicity as well as pressure from the American Civil Liberties Union and Chinese American organizations, the U.S. Immigration Service finally agreed to stop detainment procedures and to settle an immigrant's right of entry at the point of departure instead of at the point of entry (Yung, 1986, p. 81). Thousands of Chinese women were also admitted under the War Brides Act. In fact, Chinese women were the main group admitted under this act (Chan, 1991a, p. 140). Facing a 3-to-1 male-female ratio in the Chinese community, some 6,000 Chinese American soldiers married women in China and brought them back to the United States before the act expired on December 30, 1949. "Since the War Brides Act," testified Lim P. Lee before a congressional committee hearing in 1947, "every ship arriving from Hong Kong or Canton carried about 200 to 250 war brides and their dependents" (quoted in Takaki, 1989, p. 417). As a result of this massive influx of immigrants, the Chinese population rose substantially from 77,000 to 117,000 during the 1940s, a jump of just over 50% (Daniels, 1988, p. 191). The women's arrival also balanced the sex ratio: It became 1.3 to 1 by 1960, a substantial drop from the 2.8 to 1 in 1940 (Wong, 1980, pp. 520-521; Daniels, 1988, p. 191; Chan, 1991a, p. 140).

Whereas Chinese war brides married mainly co-ethnics, Japanese, Korean, and Filipino wives of GIs more often than not married non-Asian men. Most of these women entered not under the War Brides Act but as nonquota immigrants (i.e., as spouses of U.S. citizens). During the 1950s, 80% of the more than 45,000 Japanese immigrants were women, almost all of them wives of U.S. servicemen whom they had met during the postwar U.S. occupation of Japan (Nishi, 1995, p. 100). These women scattered all over the United States, leading isolated lives in the hometowns of their husbands (Strauss, 1954; Schnepp & Yui, 1955). U.S. military presence in Korea likewise produced an influx of Korean immigrants. Between the years 1950 and 1964, more than 15,000 Koreans were admitted to the United States, almost 40% of whom came as G.I. wives (Min, 1995, p. 202). The postwar years also brought a large number of Filipino immigrants. The arrival of 16,000 women—almost all wives of U.S. servicemen (including a sizable number of Filipino Americans serving in the U.S. Navy)—revitalized the Filipino American community and reduced the ratio of Filipino men to women to 3.5 to 1 (Agbayani-Siewert & Revilla, 1995). Many scholars have documented the cultural and marital adjustment of Asian military wives of non-Asian men (Strauss, 1954; Schnepp & Yui, 1955; Kim, 1972, 1977). Because this book focuses on relations between Asian American men and women, the following paragraphs review only the lives of (mostly Chinese) women who married their co-ethnics.

The male-dominant communities of Asian America were ill prepared in many ways for the influx of immigrants. Though the arrival of women and children transformed Asian America into more gender-balanced, family-oriented communities, it also exacerbated growing problems of substandard housing, underemployment, poor health conditions, and inadequate social services. Arriving in the late 1940s and early 1950s, Asian women discovered that it was well-nigh impossible—due to their limited means and race-based discrimination—to find housing outside the ethnic ghettos. Thus, for a time, many of the newly formed or reconstituted families were packed into barely furnished one- or two-room apartments, many of which had up to then housed mainly single men (Yung, 1986; Chan, 1991a, p. 141). Rose Hum Lee (1956, p. 16) reported that in the San Francisco-Oakland area, many Chinese families were forced to live in one hotel room or hastily converted bachelor's quarters with limited kitchen and bath facilities.

With their meager incomes, Asian men also had a difficult time providing for their new families. To supplement their husbands' wages, many newly arrived women worked in Chinatown restaurants and sweatshops, where they labored long hours for less than minimum wage, received no overtime or health and vacation benefits, and toiled under dangerous and unsanitary conditions. The life of Dong Zem Ping, as documented in *Sewing Woman*, a film by Arthur Dong (1982), exemplifies the hardships experienced by many Chinatown seamstresses of the post-World War II era. Married off at age 13 to a Gold Mountain man, Dong had no contact with her husband during the Sino-Japanese War and was able to join him in the United States after the war only by posing as a war bride. With limited English language and job skills, Dong could find work only as a seamstress. For the rest of her working life in the United States, she was bound to her sewing machine:

> I can still recall the times when I had one foot on the pedal and another one on an improvised rocker, rocking one son to sleep while the other was tied to my back. Many times I would accidentally sew my finger instead of the fabric because one child screamed or because I was falling asleep on the job. (quoted in Yung, 1986, p. 81)

Confronted with language barriers, cultural differences, limited economic opportunities, and the sheer pressure of daily survival, many post-World War II wives were disillusioned and disappointed with their new lives—and by extension, with their husbands. The "separated wives"—those older women who had lived apart from their husbands for many years—had the most difficult time. Though they had been married for years, these women had seen their husbands only briefly during the husbands' periodic visits; and many had not seen their husbands for 18 to 25 years. As long as the husbands provided economically for the family and the wives reared the children, the prolonged separation did not seem to threaten this "split-household" arrangement. Once reunited, however, spouses complained of incompatibility, conflicting goals and values, and "unreasonable" sexual demands. Money was a source of constant friction. Many wives were deeply disappointed in their husbands' menial jobs or the type of business they operated. They could not accept the minimal earnings, the long workdays, and the physical labor that their husbands invested in these modest enterprises. "I was so . . . shocked by our home—" declared Lee Wai Lan, who reunited with her husband and four children in 1946, "a filthy house with a small hole between two bricks for a toilet. I wanted to die." Determined to make it in the United States, Lee found a job washing dishes and peeling vegetables in a Chinese restaurant, rented a small house for her family, and later saved and borrowed enough money to start her own restaurant (Yung, 1986, p. 81). Other disillusioned wives returned to China. One wife flatly declared that she had a return plane ticket and would leave alone if her husband did not sell his business at once and reestablish himself in China (Lee, 1956, p. 23).

In these reconstituted families, husbands and wives had to renegotiate their roles and institute a new gender division of labor. In some instances, a more egalitarian division of labor emerged. For example, the domestic skills that men had been forced to learn in their wives' absence—cooking, ironing, grocery shopping—were still put to use (see Hondagneu-Sotelo, 1994, p. 113). On the other hand, the habits that some migrant husbands acquired during the separation—the drinking and gambling—stressed the family's budget and caused considerable friction between the spouses (Nakano, 1990, p. 38). The reconstituted family also threatened the authority of these "separated" wives. During the prolonged absence of their husbands, these women had assumed total family governance and spent as they deemed best the periodic but large remittances from their husbands. In the United States, these women resented having to share or relinquish their authority to their husbands, especially in the matter of household finances (Yung, 1986).

Given the brief courtship period, the war brides, like the "separated" wives, were not well acquainted with their husbands. However, younger than the latter by at least 10 years, these wives had an easier time adapting to life in the United States. In a study of war wives, Rose Hum Lee (1956) reported that the more "modern" wives wore Western-style clothes, styled their hair, adopted American names, and walked arm in arm or holding hands with their husbands in public. In these families, wives relied on husbands' "superior" knowledge of American culture and accepted the latter's choice and taste in home furnishings, clothing, and personal accessories. Following the patterns of the older immigrant men, some of the younger husbands assumed more domestic responsibilities, such as buying groceries and performing household chores. In fact, many husbands taught wives how to cook—a skill they had learned as bachelors and as restaurant cooks or kitchen helpers (Lee, 1956, p. 20). However, in the marriages that failed to thrive, the husband, with his greater social, economic, and sexual freedom, could escape through alcoholism, gambling, extramarital relations, or prolonged absence. In contrast, as women, and as newly arrived immigrants who possessed limited English language and job skills, their wives had fewer forms of escapism available to them and often had to confine their frustrations, anxieties, and hostilities within the family (Lee, 1956, p. 21).

The influx of women immigrants in the late 1940s produced a Chinese American baby boom. Like the second-generation Asian Americans of the 1930s and 1940s, many young Chinese American women growing up in the 1950s experienced race-based and culture-based gender discrimination. In many Chinese families, sons continued to receive preferential treatment over daughters. "When we were growing up," complained Bettie Luke Kan of Seattle of the double standards in her family,

> Marge and I had to work part-time, applying for scholarships, and pay our own way. But with Robert [brother], it was like, "Do you need more money?" It was just constant. He could go to the movies, play with friends, go downtown, and have spending money. Marge and I—in those growing up years when we had the grocery store—we were allowed one movie a year on New Year's Day; that was it. (cited in Yung, 1986, p. 88)

These young women also had to combat sexist stereotypes of Asian American women in the media, particularly the image of the sexy, submissive prostitute popularized by Nancy Kwan in the 1960 film *The World of Suzie Wong* (see Chapter 5). Besieged by mass media images that constructed and reinforced U.S. standards of beauty as "blond, blue eyed, and big breasted," young Chinese American women of the 1950s received a message of inferiority from the larger society as strong as that which they received at home (Yung, 1986, p. 88).

Political refugees composed the final group of Asians who came in under special legislation during the post-World War II period. After the Communist victory in China in 1949, some 23,000 highly educated and well-trained Chinese men and women were granted political asylum in the United States under the 1948 Displaced Persons Act and the 1953 Refugee Relief Act. Primarily Mandarin speakers from central and northern China, these refugees were some of China's brightest intellectuals, most of whom were from well-to-do families (Chan, 1991a, p. 141). Their educational background, ability to speak English, and previous exposure to Western ideas eased their integration into U.S. society. Due to the high demand for their scientific and technical skills, these men and women found work in academic and professional fields. Because of dialect and class differences, this new group bought homes in the suburbs away from the impoverished Chinatowns and seldom associated with the old-time Chinese immigrants (Yung, 1986, p. 82). Their presence augmented the Chinese American middle class and further bifurcated the Chinese American community along class lines.

Conclusion

World War II and the postwar years brought significant changes to the lives of Asians in the United States, all of which led to shifting roles of men and women. The wartime internment, for example, resulted in the subversion of male dominance over women and parental authority over children in the Japanese American communities. The internment years stripped Issei men of their role as the family breadwinner and transferred some of the power and status to their U.S.-born children. The camp experience also decreased male dominance over women, as older Issei women gained more leisure time and younger Nisei women found unprecedented job opportunities in the camp enterprises and service divisions. After the war, these role changes persisted as Issei men faced limited job opportunities while their college-educated children moved into predominantly white-collar, managerial, and professional occupations. In other Asian American communities, particularly the Chinese American community, the influx of women and the subsequent (re)establishment of conjugal families "created havoc, throwing the male dominant community out of kilter" (Hsiao, 1992, p. 152). As the Chinatown community changed from a community of aging bachelors to a community of young families, husbands and wives had to renegotiate their gender roles—a process that led at times to a more egalitarian division of labor. Although the postwar immigrants brought new vitality into Asian American communities, family separation was to remain common until the immigration reform of 1965.

Notes

1. Manzanar Camp, located in Owens, California, was the first of the permanent concentration camps to open in 1942.

2. In Hawaii, just over 1,400, or less than 1%, of the territory's Japanese were interned (Okihiro, 1991).

3. Xiaojian Zhao (in press) has estimated that by 1943, about 5,000 Chinese Americans were working (or had worked) for defense-related industries in the San Francisco Bay Area and that between 500 to 600 of them were women. Most of these working women were second-generation daughters of immigrant women.

CHAPTER 4

Contemporary Asian America

Immigration, Increasing Diversity, and Changing Resources

As indicated in Chapter 2, exclusion laws restricted Asian immigration to the United States, skewed the sex ratio of the early communities, and truncated the development of conjugal families. The 1965 Immigration Act ended this exclusion and equalized immigration rights for all nationalities. No longer constrained by exclusion laws, Asian immigrants—most of whom come from countries deeply affected by U.S. colonialism, war, and neocolonialism— began arriving in much larger numbers than ever before. In the period from 1971 to 1990, approximately 855,500 Filipinos, 610,800 Koreans, and 576,100 Chinese entered the United States (U.S. Bureau of the Census, 1992). Moreover, with the collapse of U.S.-backed governments in South Vietnam, Laos, and Cambodia in 1975, over 1 million escapees from these countries resettled in the United States. As a consequence, in the 1980s, Asia was the largest source of U.S. legal immigrants, accounting for 40% to 47% of the total influx. After Mexico, the Philippines and South Korea were the second- and third-largest source countries of immigrants. Three other Asian countries—China, India, and Vietnam—were among the 10 major source countries of U.S. immigrants in the 1980s (Min, 1995, p. 12).

Fueled by the influx of Asian immigrants, the Asian American population doubled from 1.5 million in 1970 to 3.7 million in 1980 and to 7.3 million in 1990. In 1990, 66% of Asians in the United States were foreign born (U.S. Bureau of the Census, 1993, p. 3, Figure 3). The post-1965 Asian arrivals differ from the earlier immigrants in at least three respects. In contrast to the largely unskilled immigrant population of the pre-World War II period, the new arrivals include not only low-wage service-sector workers but also significant numbers of white-collar professionals. The majority arrive as families intending permanent settlement rather than as sojourning single men. According to the

Immigration and Naturalization Service data for the fiscal years 1988 to 1990, close to 75% of professional immigrants from Asia came with their families (Kanjanapan, 1995, p. 19). Southeast Asian refugees also came to the United States as part of a family. One survey found that about 87% of the Vietnamese, 71% of the Cambodians, and 81% of the Hmongs fled with their families (Rumbaut, 1995, p. 256). Finally, whereas the old immigration was composed mostly of men, the contemporary flow is female dominated.

Reflecting sociologists' concerns with economic issues and the structures of immigrant opportunity in the United States, most studies of post-1965 Asian America have focused on Asian American relations with and adaptation to the larger society rather than on relations among group members. With a few notable exceptions, we have little information on family and gender relations within these emerging communities. Existing data indicate some changes in gender relations as a result of migration and suggest that Asian women's ability to challenge traditional patriarchy rests on the dependence of Asian men on the economic and social resources of women (see Kibria, 1993). Given the sizable literature on socioeconomic adaptation and the connections between work and gender dynamics, I divide the following discussion into three economic categories and examine gender relations within each group: the highly educated, the disadvantaged, and the entrepreneurs. Certainly, these three categories are neither mutually exclusive nor exhaustive. They are also linked in the sense that there is mobility between them, particularly from the professions to small-business employment (Chen, 1992, p. 142). Nevertheless, they represent perhaps the most important sociological groupings within the contemporary Asian American community (Ong & Hee, 1994, p. 31). As in the previous chapters, the focus here is on relations between Asian American men and women rather than on Asian American women themselves or their relations with white men and white women.

Changing Laws, Labor Needs, and Gender Composition

The United States today attracts proportionally more female immigrants than do most other immigrant-receiving nations. Women constitute the clear majority among U.S. immigrants from nations in Asia, but also in Central and South America, the Caribbean, and Europe (Donato, 1992). A majority are married, and most arrive as workers (Sacks &

Scheper-Hughes, 1987, p. 176). The dominance of women in immigration flows reflects the growth of female-intensive industries in the United States, particularly in service, health care, microelectronics, and apparel manufacturing. To escape the tightening labor market, employers in the United States (and also in other "developed" countries) have opted either to shift labor-intensive processes to less-developed countries or to import migrant labor, especially female labor to fill low-wage, insecure assembly and service-sector jobs (Lim, 1983, p. 84; Hossfeld, 1994). Women thus have become a rapidly growing segment of the world's migratory and international workforce (Sacks & Scheper-Hughes, 1987, p. 176).

Between 1975 and 1980, women (20 years and older) constituted more than 50% of the immigrants from China, Burma, Indonesia, Taiwan, Hong Kong, Malaysia, the Philippines, Korea, Japan, and Thailand (Donato, 1992). The dual goals of the 1965 Immigration Act—to facilitate family reunification and to admit skilled workers needed by the U.S. economy—have dramatically increased the number of Asian women immigrants[1] (Donato & Tyree, 1986). Women who came as wives, daughters, or mothers of U.S. permanent residents and citizens constitute the primary component of change. Since 1965, most visas have been allocated to relatives of U.S. residents (Donato, 1992, p. 164). Regardless of their status as family immigrants, once in the United States, Asian immigrant women have been as strongly motivated as immigrant men to work. Due to the lower earnings of their husbands, the majority of recent immigrant women have entered the labor force. In the United States, the labor force participation of immigrant women surpasses that of the native born, and Asian American women have recorded the most active involvement in employment (Gardner, Robey, & Smith, 1985). In 1980, among married immigrant women between the ages of 25 and 64 years, 61% of Korean women, 65% of Chinese women, and 83% of Filipina women were in the labor force (Duleep & Sanders, 1993). In 1990, Asian women had a slightly higher labor force participation rate than all women, 60% and 57% respectively (U.S. Bureau of the Census, 1993, p. 5, Figure 6).

The 1965 act also allowed women to enter the United States as occupational immigrants. Whereas most of the Asian women who immigrated before World War II were of working-class origin and acquired jobs primarily in the secondary sector, the contemporary immigrant women came from heterogeneous backgrounds and entered a wide range of occupational fields. Because the 1965 act gives a higher preference to professional-level workers, Asian immigrant women have had more opportunities to acquire jobs in the primary sector than before (Chow, 1994). Among Filipino and Korean immigrants, more females than males were admitted in recent years under the third preference of the 1965 Immigration Act—the preference reserved for professional immigrants and their families. This female predominance reflects the movement of women medical professionals to the United States to alleviate this country's recurring shortage of doctors, nurses, and other health-related practitioners (Asis, 1991; Ong & Azores, 1994b). Just as the early Asian immigrants were recruited for farm labor, by the 1970s recent medical graduates in Asia, particularly in the Philippines, were recruited to work in U.S. hospitals, nursing homes, and health organizations (Pido, 1986, p. 85). The passage of the Immigration Nurses Act in 1989, which offered permanent residency to foreign nurses who had lived and worked in the United States in the recent past, further ensures at least a short-term increase in women's presence among legal immigrants (Donato, 1992, p. 181). In addition, an unknown number of single Asian women came to study in the United States, married U.S. citizens, and stayed after their schooling was completed; others stayed to work in U.S. companies and universities. This "brain drain" phenomenon, especially among Asian Indian and Filipina women, challenges the assumption that female immigrants are automatically placed in the peripheral sector (Yamanaka & McClelland, 1994, p. 86).

Asian Americans and the
Contemporary U.S. Labor Market

The new Asian immigrants entered a U.S. labor market that, though still growing, encountered numerous problems by the end of the 1960s. Since World War II, global capitalism has undergone considerable growth and change. This restructuring—rapid global economic integration—eroded the postwar dominance of the United States in the world economy, resulting in stagnation, a slowdown in productivity growth, high inflation, rising unemployment, and economic dislocation (Ong, Bonacich, & Cheng, 1994). In the early 1980s, the United States suffered the worst recession since the Great Depression. Unemployment increased from an annual average of 4.8% in the 1960s to 7.3% in the 1980s. This restructuring led to a decrease in the number of high-paying manufacturing jobs in the U.S. labor market and an increase in the number of poorly paid as well as highly paid jobs in the service sector (Mar & Kim, 1994, pp. 23-24).

Relative to earlier historical periods, the employment pattern of today's Asian Americans is considerably more varied, a result of both the 1965 Immigration Act and the restructured economy. As discussed earlier, during the first half of the century, Asians were concentrated at the bottom of the economic ladder, restricted to retailing, food service, menial service, and agricultural occupations. After World War II, economic opportunities improved, but not sufficiently for educated Asian Americans to achieve parity. In the post-1965 era, the economic status of Asian Americans has bifurcated, showing some great improvements but also persistent problems. Today's Asian Americans both join whites in the well-paid, educated, white-collar sector of the workforce (albeit as "proletarianized" professionals)[2] *and* join Latino immigrants in lower-paying service and manufacturing jobs (Ong & Hee, 1994). Responding to limited job opportunities for highly skilled immigrants, a large number of Asian immigrants have also turned to self-employment (Ong & Hee, 1994). Situating gender relations within these three economic groupings, the following discussion explores the connections between wage earning and changing perceptions of gender roles and status within the contemporary Asian American community.

The Highly Educated

According to the 1990 U.S. census, 43% of Asian men and 32% of Asian women 25 years of age and over had at least a bachelor's degree, compared with 23% and 17% respectively of the total U.S. population (U.S. Bureau of the Census, 1993, p. 4). Moreover, the proportion of Asians with a graduate or professional degree was higher than that of whites: 14% versus 8% (Ong & Hee, 1994). However, as indicated in Table 4.1, the educational attainment of different Asian groups varied widely: Asian Indians had the highest attainment rates and Hmong the lowest. In 1990, close to 66% of Asian Indian men and 49% of Asian Indian women had graduated with a bachelor's degree or higher, compared with 7% for Hmong men and 3% for Hmong women (U.S. Bureau of the Census, 1993, p. 4, Table 1). Immigrants account for about two thirds to three quarters of the highly educated population (Ong & Hee, 1994, pp. 38-39). During the fiscal years 1988 to 1990, of the more than 150,000 professional immigrants who came to the United States from throughout the world, slightly over half (51.5%) came from Asia (Kanjanapan, 1995, p. 15). Asian immigrant men dominated all professional occupations, particularly in the fields of engineering, mathematics,

TABLE 4.1

Educational Attainment of Bachelor's Degree or Higher by Sex and Ethnicity: 1990

	Male	Female
Total population	23.3	17.6
Total Asian	43.2	32.7
Chinese	46.7	35.0
Filipino	36.2	41.6
Japanese	42.6	28.2
Asian Indian	65.7	48.7
Korean	46.9	25.9
Vietnamese	22.3	12.2
Cambodian	8.6	3.2
Hmong	7.0	3.0
Laotian	7.0	3.5
Thai	47.7	24.9
Other Asian	47.5	34.2

SOURCE: U.S. Bureau of the Census, 1993, p. 4, Table 1.

and computer science, and Asian immigrant women constituted the majority in health care (Kanjanapan, 1995).

Asian Americans, bolstered by the immigration of scientists and engineers (S&E), have contributed more to the technological capacity of the United States than any other minority group. In 1990, Asians were 3% of the U.S. total population but accounted for close to 7% of the S&E labor force. Their greatest presence is among engineers with a doctorate degree, constituting over one fifth of this group in 1980 and in 1990. Chinese constituted the largest group (34%) of Asian American S&Es, followed by Asian Indians (23%), Japanese (12%), and Filipinos (10%; Ong & Blumenberg, 1994, p. 169).

In the field of health care, two thirds of foreign nurses and 60% of foreign doctors admitted to the United States during the fiscal years 1988 to 1990 were from Asia (Kanjanapan, 1995, p. 18). Today, Asians represent nearly a quarter of the health care providers in public hospitals in major U.S. metropolitan areas (Ong & Azores, 1994a, p. 139). The Philippines is the largest supplier of health professionals to the United

States, sending nearly 25,000 nurses to this country between 1966 and 1985 and another 10,000 between 1989 and 1991 (Ong & Azores, 1994a, p. 154). Due to the shortage of nurses in the United States, women have dominated the Filipino immigrant population since 1960. This dominance of professional women, in part, reflects the relatively high status of women in the Philippines. In contrast to the patriarchal, patrilineal, and patrilocal nature of Chinese, Japanese, and Korean societies, the gender structure in the Philippines is more egalitarian, and kinship is bilateral (Pido, 1986, p. 23). In employment as well as in participation in economic, political, and social activities, Filipina women had and continue to have more or less equal status with men (Pido, 1986, p. 23). Luz Latus, a Filipina nurse in the United States, recalled the high aspirations that her father had for her: "He would have liked to see me become a teacher, a doctor, or a lawyer" (Espiritu, 1995, p. 29). As of the mid-1970s, the Philippines was one of the few countries in the world where the number of women in postsecondary education equaled or exceeded that of men (Castillo, 1979; Pido, 1986, p. 82). In particular, women constituted the majority in all health-related professions except for medicine, where the numbers of male and female physicians were nearly equal (Pido, 1986, pp. 78-82; also Castillo, 1979). As indicated in Table 4.1, Filipina women were the only female group that had a higher proportion of college graduates than their male counterparts did: 41.6% versus 36.2% in 1990 (U.S. Bureau of the Census, 1993, p. 4, Table 1).

Despite their superior levels of education, Asian American men still receive lower economic returns than white men. In 1990, highly educated Asian American men who worked full time, full year, earned about 10% less than white men—even though the former were much more likely to have a graduate degree. Moreover, Asian American men were considerably less likely than white men to hold a job as an executive, administrator, or manager (23% versus 31%). Among highly educated females, both Asian American and white women faced a gender gap, earning only about 70% of the salaries of white men with similar backgrounds. But Asian American women fared worse than their white counterparts: 31% of Asian Americans were professionals compared with 48% of whites, and 19% of Asian Americans were in the managerial class compared with 23% of whites (Ong & Hee, 1994, pp. 40-41).

Asian men also earned more money than Asian women for each level of education. In 1990, men with a doctorate degree earned a median income of $50,000, whereas women with the same degree made only $34,000. Asian men and women also differed in occupational standing. With the exception of Filipina nurses, there tended to be a higher percentage of males (31%) in the professional and managerial class than of females (24%; Ong & Azores, 1994a; Ong & Hee, 1994, pp. 40-41). Among Korean-born and -educated physicians in the United States, female physicians are more likely than male physicians to enter the peripheral specialties of American medicine—the low-income-producing and less competitive fields. Shin and Chang (1988) contended that the Korean female physician was peripheralized "not only as an immigrant but also as a woman" (p. 621).

The above statistics indicate that racism and sexism continue to affect the distribution of economic resources in the United States. As female workers of color, Asian American women experience their work world not just as gendered but also as racialized individuals. They are more likely to remain marginalized in their work organization, to encounter a "glass ceiling," and to earn less than white men, Asian American men, and white women with comparable educational back-grounds (Yamanaka & McClelland, 1994, p. 86). They also are more likely to be underemployed. In 1970, a third of U.S.-born, college-educated Chinese American women were in clerical work. In 1980, close to a third of U.S.-born Filipinas with 4 or more years of college occupied clerical positions (Woo, 1985, p. 331). Similarly, Chai (1987) reported that an estimated 60% of college-educated Korean women immigrants in Hawaii experienced a drop in occupational status into service jobs (pp. 225-226). Chai attributed this underemployment primarily to racial and gender discrimination and to the strict licensing procedures for foreign-educated professionals. In an analysis of the occupational pat-terns of Asian American women, Yamanaka and McClelland (1994) reached a similar conclusion: "Asian American women, both native and foreign born, as of 1980, have not yet escaped the stigmatization of being minority and recent immigrants in a discriminatory market" (p. 108). The experiences of W. W. Tom, an electronics assembler, exemplify the lives of many under- and misemployed professionals. Once a physicist in China, Tom came to the United States in 1976. Because of language barriers, she was unable to find work in her profession. Regarding her predicament and that of others like her, she said,

> We are all college graduates, but working in sewing or electronics factories. We all have taken a big step backwards in our profession or work, but we are lucky to find work—any work that we can do. I would be happy if I could just advance myself at my present job one step up.

I have thought about this constantly . . . the day when I can work at a
desk using a pen and not have to do menial labor. (cited in Yung, 1986,
p. 107)

What can these socioeconomic patterns tell us about gender relations between highly educated Asian American men and women?
Because we have little information on the connections between work
and home life—between the public and private spheres—of this population, the following discussion is necessarily exploratory. Employed as
professionals (albeit in lower-status and lower-salary positions), most
highly educated Asian American women need not rely exclusively on
their husbands for economic survival. Their earnings provide them
with a bargaining chip to negotiate for greater male involvement in
household labor (Hood, 1983; Kibria, 1993; Pesquera, 1993; Hondagneu-
Sotelo, 1994). According to a national survey of college-educated
women from India living in the United States, 33.3% of the women
working in technical fields and 50% in academic fields described themselves as feminists (Dasgupta, 1985, pp. 15-17). In a study of Taiwan
immigrants in New York, Hsiang-Shui Chen (1992) reported that the
degree of husbands' participation in household labor varied considerably along class lines, with men in the professional class doing a greater
share than men in the working and small-business classes. Although
women still performed most of the household labor, men helped with
vacuuming, disposing of garbage, laundry, dishwashing, and bath-
room cleaning (p. 77). Beatriz M. Pesquera (1993) found a similar division of household labor among Chicano professionals: "Professional
men married to professional women did a greater share than most other
men" (p. 194). Pesquera attributed this more equitable household division of labor to the lack of a substantial earning gap between professional men and women, the demands of the women's careers, and
women's ability to pressure their husbands into doing their share of the
household chores (p. 194). However, both Chen and Pesquera reiter-
ated that these marriages are not egalitarian in household chore alloca-
tion. Although professional families have moved toward less sex-role-
segregated arrangements, women still perform more of the household
labor than their husbands. Moreover, Pesquera reported that for the
most part, the only way women have altered the distribution of household labor has been through conflict and confrontation, suggesting that
ideologically most men continue to view housework as women's work
(p. 185). These two case studies remind us that professional women, like

most other working women, have to juggle full-time work outside the home with the responsibilities of child care and housework. This burden is magnified for professional women because most tend to live in white, suburban neighborhoods where they have little or no access to the women's social networks that exist in highly connected ethnic communities (Glenn, 1983, p. 41; Kibria, 1993).

Given the shortage of medical personnel in the United States, particularly in the inner cities and in rural areas, women health professionals seem to be in the best position to challenge traditional patriarchy. First, as a much sought-after group among U.S. immigrants, Asian women health practitioners can enter the United States as the principal immigrants (Espiritu, 1995, p. 21). This means that unmarried women can immigrate on their own accord and that married women can enter as the primary immigrants, with their husbands and children following as dependents. A female-first migration stream, especially when the women are married, has enormous ramifications for both family relations and domestic roles. For example, when Joey Laguda's mother, a medical technologist, entered the country, she carried the primary immigrant status and sponsored Joey's father and two other sons as her dependents. Joey describes the downward occupational shift that his father experienced on immigrating to the United States: "My father had graduated in the Philippines with a bachelor's degree in criminology but couldn't get a job as a police officer here because he was not a U.S. citizen. So he only worked blue-collar jobs" (Espiritu, 1995, p. 181). The experience of Joey's father suggests that Asian men who immigrate as their wives' dependents often have to subordinate their careers, at least initially, to those of their wives. Moreover, given the long hours and the graveyard shifts that typify a nurse's work schedule, many men have had to assume more child care and other household responsibilities in their wives' absences. A survey of Filipina nurses in Los Angeles County reveals that these women, to increase their incomes, tend to work double shifts or in the higher-paying evening and night shifts (Ong & Azores, 1994b, pp. 183-184). Finally, unlike most other women professionals, Asian American nurses often work among their co-ethnics and thus benefit from these social support systems. According to Paul Ong and Tania Azores (1994b), there are "visible clusterings of Filipino nurses" in many hospitals in large metropolitan areas (p. 187). These women's social networks can provide the emotional and material support needed to challenge male authority.

Last, racism in the workplace threatens the employment security and class status of Asian American professionals and places undue stress on the family. Singh, a mechanical engineer who immigrated to the United States from India in 1972, became discouraged when he was not advancing at the same rate as his colleagues and attributed his difficulties to job discrimination based on national and racial origins. Singh's wife, Kaur, describes how racism affected her husband and her family: "It became harder and harder for my husband to put up with the discrimination at work. He was always stressed out. This affected the whole family. The thing about the discrimination that always seemed weird was that he kept getting raises in terms of money but no promotions" (quoted in Dhaliwal, 1995, p. 78).

The Disadvantaged

The contemporary Asian American community also includes a sizable population with limited education, skills, and English-speaking ability. In 1990, 18% of Asian men and 26% of Asian women age 25 and over in the United States had less than a high school degree. Also, of the 4.1 million Asians 5 years and over, 56% did not speak English "very well," and 35% were linguistically isolated (U.S. Bureau of the Census, 1993, Table 2). The median income for those with limited English was $20,000 for males and $15,600 for females; for those with less than a high school degree, the figures were $18,000 and $15,000 respectively. Asian American men and women with both limited English-speaking ability and low levels of education fared the worst. For a large portion of this disadvantaged population, even working full time, full year, brought in less than $10,000 in earnings (Ong & Hee, 1994, p. 45).

As with the highly educated, the disadvantaged population is largely a product of immigration: Nine tenths are immigrants (Ong & Hee, 1994). The majority enter the United States as relatives of the pre-1965 Asian immigrants. Because new immigrants tend to have socioeconomic backgrounds similar to those of their sponsors, most family reunification immigrants represent a continuation of the unskilled and semiskilled Asian labor that emigrated before 1965 (Liu, Ong, & Rosenstein, 1991). The immigration history of the Singh family of Stanislaus County, California, provides an example. The first immigrant in Mr. Singh's family was his sister, who had married a man whose father had entered California in the early 1900s as a farm laborer. Taking advantage of the family reunification provisions in the 1965 Immigration Act, she sponsored Mr. Singh (her brother), who in turn sponsored his wife. In Stanislaus County, Mr. Singh found a job as a forklift driver for a large food-processing plant while his wife worked in the fields picking various crops (Williams, 1989, pp. 151-152).

Southeast Asian refugees, particularly the second-wave refugees who arrived after 1978, represent another largely disadvantaged group. In a study of the economic progress of 11 different immigrant groups, Chiswick (1979) concluded that refugees face the steepest barriers in achieving economic success. This is so because refugees are less likely to be a self-selected labor force than economic migrants. Instead, their numbers include many unemployables: young children, the elderly, religious and political leaders, and people in poor mental and physical condition (Portes & Rumbaut, 1990). They are also less likely to have acquired readily transferable skills and are more likely to have made investments (in training and education) specific to the country of origin (Chiswick, 1979; Montero, 1980). For example, there are significant numbers of Southeast Asian military personnel with skills for which there is no longer a market in the United States. In 1990, the overall economic status of the Southeast Asian population was characterized by unstable, minimum-wage employment, welfare dependency, and participation in the informal economy (Gold & Kibria, 1993). They have the highest percentage with less than a high school degree (64%) and with limited English-speaking ability (55%), the highest rates of jobless-ness of any Asian American group (33% for males and 58% for females), and the highest welfare dependency rates of any ethnic or racial group in the United States (Ong & Umemoto, 1994, p. 109). Poverty is also severe for these populations: 10% of Vietnamese and 16% of Cambodi-ans and Laotians live on annual incomes of only $6,307, less than 50% of the poverty threshold (Ong, 1993, pp. 15-16). These statistics call attention to the danger of lumping all Asian groups together because Southeast Asians—and other disadvantaged groups—do not share in the relatively favorable socioeconomic outcomes attributed to the "av-erage" Asian American.

Lacking the skills and education to catapult them into the primary sector of the economy, disadvantaged Asian American men and women work in the secondary labor market: the labor-intensive, low-capital service, and small manufacturing sectors. The typical pattern of a dual-worker family is a husband who works as a waiter, cook, janitor, or store helper and a wife who is employed in a garment shop or on an assembly line. In a recent survey conducted by the Asian Immigrant Women Advocates, 93% of the 166 seamstresses surveyed listed their husbands' jobs as unskilled or semiskilled, including waiter, busboy, gardener, day laborer, and the like (Louie, 1992, p. 9). Most disadvantaged male immigrants can get jobs only in ethnic businesses in which wages are low but only simple English is required (Chen, 1992, p. 103). A waiter employed in a Chinatown restaurant usually earns about $200 a month, with no overtime pay, no health benefits, and no job security (Ong, 1984).

Disadvantaged women seem to have more employment options than men. The garment industry is a top employer of immigrant women. Women's dual responsibility of supplementing household income and of maintaining the home contributes to their heavy concentration in the garment industry. The industry's informal work style allows mothers to supervise their children at the job site or to work at home. Flexible work hours also allow workers to complete family errands (Ong, 1984, p. 51). Today, Asian immigrant women, particularly Chinese, Koreans, and Vietnamese, are an important component of the U.S. garment labor force. Exploiting this supply of immigrant female labor, the garment industry has transformed the Chinatowns of New York City and San Francisco into industrial centers specializing in clothing production (Takaki, 1989, p. 427).

Asian immigrant women are also overrepresented in the microelectronics industry. Of the more than 200,000 people employed in the California's Silicon Valley electronics industry in 1980, 50% were involved in production-related jobs. Women constitute about 80% to 90% of the workers who assemble the integrated circuits for computers, radios, televisions, watches, stereos, microwave ovens, calculators, and other electronic equipment. As many as half of these assembly workers are recent immigrants from the Philippines, Vietnam, Korea, and South Asia. In this largely nonunion industry, the assembly workers labor for minimum wage under hazardous, stressful, and unstable working conditions (Mazumdar, 1989, p. 19; Villones, 1989, p. 176; Hossfeld, 1994, pp. 71-72). In many electronics corporations, wages and promotions are structured along racial and gender lines, with men and white workers earning higher wages and being much more likely to be promoted than women and workers of color (Villones, 1989; Hossfeld, 1994). Williams (1989) reported the same racial and gender segregation in the canning industry in Central California. Although there are no officially designated "male" and "female" jobs, overall, white men occupy the upper job brackets and women of color the lower. For example, even after a decade of reform measures, in 1984, Punjabi Sikh women employed at Tri/Valley Growers still made up the majority of the less skilled, lower paying job brackets (Williams, 1989, p. 156). In most of the departments, but especially in the preparation and canning departments, the work is subdivided into minute and repetitive tasks. Hour after hour, day after day, women on the lines stand alongside the conveyor belt; their sole task is identifying and discarding the bad fruit. One woman cannery worker describes the effects of her monotonous job: "I hate standing all day. It's noisy, it gives me a headache. The line makes me dizzy; and sometimes I get sick" (Williams, 1989, p. 154). These dreary conditions are especially unbearable during the peak season, July to mid-September, when workers toil as many as 10 hours a day, with only two 12-minute breaks and a half-hour lunch, 6 or 7 days a week (Williams, 1989, pp. 154-155).

In these labor-intensive industries—garment, microelectronics, and cannery—immigrant women, as racialized and feminized labor, are more employable than men due to the patriarchal and racist assumptions that women can afford to work for less, do not mind dead-end jobs, and are more suited physiologically to certain kinds of detailed and routine work. As Linda Lim (1983) observed, it is the "*comparative disadvantage* of women in the wage-labor market that gives them a comparative advantage vis-à-vis men in the occupations and industries where they are concentrated—so-called female ghettoes of employment" (p. 78). A white male production manager and hiring supervisor in a California Silicon Valley assembly shop discusses his formula for hiring:

> Just three things I look for in hiring [entry-level, high-tech manufacturing operatives]: small, foreign, and female. You find those three things and you're pretty much automatically guaranteed the right kind of work force. These little foreign gals are grateful to be hired—very, very grateful—no matter what. (Hossfeld, 1994, p. 65).

In Hawaii, Korean immigrant women likewise had an easier time securing employment than men because of their domestic skills and because of the demand for service workers in restaurants, hotels, hospitals, and factories (Chai, 1987, p. 77). These examples illustrate the interconnections of race, class, and gender. On the one hand, patriarchal and racist ideologies consign women to a secondary and inferior position in the capitalist wage-labor market. On the other hand, their very disadvantage—and the increased "racialized feminization of labor" in the global restructuring of capitalism (Lowe, 1996)—enhances women's employability over men in certain industries, thus affording them an opportunity to strengthen their claims against patriarchal authority in their homes.

The discussion thus far suggests at least two shifts in the resources of immigrant men and women. First, disadvantaged immigrant women are more employable than men. Second, due to the significant decline in the economic contributions of immigrant men, women's earnings make up an equal or greater share of the family income. Because the wage each earns is low, only by pooling incomes can a husband and wife earn enough to support a family (Glenn, 1983, p. 42). In a survey of Chinese American garment workers, Loo and Ong (1982) found that about 80% of the families in their sample would "barely get by" if there was only one income earner (p. 81). Both of these shifts in resources have challenged the patriarchal authority of Asian men. Men's loss of status and power, not only in the public but also in the domestic arena, places severe pressure on their sense of well-being, leading in some instances to spousal abuse and divorce (Luu, 1989, p. 68). A Korean immigrant man described his frustrations over changing gender roles and expectations:

> In Korea [my wife] used to have breakfast ready for me. . . . She didn't do it anymore because she said she was too busy getting ready to go to work. If I complained she talked back at me, telling me to fix my own breakfast. . . . I was very frustrated about her, started fighting and hit her. (Yim, 1978, quoted in Mazumdar, 1989, p. 18)

According to a 1979 survey, marital conflict was one of the top four problems of Vietnamese refugees in the United States (Davidson, 1979, cited in Luu, 1989, p. 69). A Vietnamese man, recently divorced after 10 years of marriage, blamed his wife's new roles and newfound freedom for their breakup:

> Back in the country, my role was only to bring home money from work, and my wife would take care of the household. Now everything has changed. My wife had to work as hard as I did to support the family. Soon after, she demanded more power at home. In other words, she wanted equal partnership. I am so disappointed! I realized that things are different now, but I could not help feeling the way I do. It is hard to get rid of or change my principles and beliefs which are deeply rooted in me. (Luu, 1989, p. 69)

Loss of status and power has similarly led to depression and anxieties in Hmong males. In particular, the women's ability—and the men's inability—to earn money for households "has undermined severely male omnipotence" (Irby & Pon, 1988, p. 112). Male unhappiness and helplessness can be detected in the following joke told at a family picnic: "When we get on the plane to go back to Laos, the first thing we will do is beat up the women!" The joke—which generated laughter from both men and women—drew upon a combination of "the men's unemployability, the sudden economic value placed on women's work, and men's fear of losing power in their families" (Donnelly, 1994, pp. 74-75).

The shifts in the resources of men and women have created an opportunity for women to contest the traditional hierarchies of family life. Williams (1989) reported that as wage earners, Punjabi women cannery workers have gained more control and decision-making power within their households. One woman said of her increased power within the family: "Now my husband, he listens to me when I say something; when I want to buy something, I do; and when I want to go in the car, I go" (p. 157). Ethnographic studies of Vietnamese families in Philadelphia and Korean families in Hawaii reveal the same pattern: Women's entry into the workforce enhances egalitarianism within the domestic sphere (Chai, 1987; Kibria, 1993). Existing data indicate, however, that working-class Asian immigrant women have not used their new resources to radically restructure the old family system, only to redefine it in a more satisfying manner (Kibria, 1993). Some cultural conceptions, such as the belief that the male should be the head of the household, remain despite the economic contributions of women. Nancy Donnelly (1994) reported that although Hmong women contribute the profits of their needlework sales to the family economy, the traditional construction of Hmong women as "creators of beauty, skilled in devotion to their families, and embedded in a social order dominated by men" has not changed (Donnelly, 1994, p. 185). In the following quote, a Cambodian wife describes her reluctance to upset her husband's authority:

> If we lived in Cambodia I would have behaved differently toward my husband. Over there we have to always try to be nice to the husband. Wives don't talk back, but sometimes I do that here a little bit, because I have more freedom to say what I think here. However, I am careful not to speak too disrespectfully to him, and in that way, I think I am different from the Americans. (Welaratna, 1993, p. 233)

The traditional division of household labor also remains relatively intact. In a study of Chinatown women, Loo and Ong (1982) found that despite their employment outside the home, three fourths of the working mothers were solely responsible for all household chores. In her study of Vietnamese American families, Kibria (1993) argued that Vietnamese American women (and children) walk an "ideological tightrope"—struggling both to preserve the traditional Vietnamese family system and to enhance their power within the context of this system. According to Kibria, the traditional family system is valuable to Vietnamese American women because it offers them economic protection and gives them authority, as mothers, over the younger generation.

For disadvantaged Asian Americans, then, the family, and the traditional patriarchy within it, becomes simultaneously a bastion of resistance to race and class oppression and an instrument for gender subordination (Glenn, 1986, p. 193). Constrained by their social-structural location in the dominant society, disadvantaged Asian women may accept certain components of the old male-dominant system to have a strong and intact family—an important source of support to sustain them in the work world (Morokvasic, 1984, pp. 894-895; Glenn, 1986, p. 193). Women also preserve the traditional family system, though in a tempered form, because they value the promise of male economic protection. Although migration may have equalized the economic resources of working-class men and women, women's earnings continue to be too meager to sustain their economic independence from men (Kibria, 1990). Finally, like many ethnic, immigrant, poor, and working-class women, disadvantaged Asian women view work as an opportunity to raise the family's living standards and not as the path to fulfillment or even upward mobility idealized by the white feminist movement. As such, employment is defined as an extension of their family obligations—of their roles as mothers and wives (Kim & Hurh, 1988, p. 162; Pedraza, 1991; Romero, 1992). For example, the Punjabi women cannery workers do not view work and family as incompatible, dichotomized spheres. Mrs. Singh describes the interconnection of these two spheres: "My work is my family, you know, with all my relatives and friends there; and, of course, my family is my work" (Williams, 1989, p. 157). Nearly all the Punjabi women emphasize that they work outside the home to contribute to their families' welfare—with most hoping to help finance the family goal of purchasing a small plot of orchard land (Williams, 1989).

The Self-Employed

As in the previous historical periods, Asian Americans have created their own solution to labor market barriers through small-business development. Business ownership is appealing because it offers the prospect of financial security, independence, and the opportunity to employ family members (Gold, 1988). Between 1972 and 1987, the number of Asian American-owned businesses grew 973% (from 33,114 to 355,331), as compared with 252% for Latinos and 118% for African Americans. By 1987, in terms of sales and number of employees, Asian American businesses also fared better than Latino and African American businesses (Ong & Hee, 1994, p. 48). Koreans have the highest self-employment rate of any immigrant group (Light & Bonacich, 1986). On the basis of a 1986 survey, 53% of Korean male workers in Los Angeles and 36% of female workers were self-employed. Besides the 45% who were self-employed, another 30% worked in the Korean ethnic market. These figures indicate that three out of four Korean workers were employed in the Korean ethnic economy (Min, 1995, p. 209). A predeparture survey of Korean women who emigrated in 1986 indicated that 30% expected to become self-employed in the United States. However, much of the expected rate in self-employment was related to the business intentions of their husbands; only a few women intended to start a business of their own (Asis, 1991, p. 37).

The Asian American self-employed population is also largely a product of immigration: 85% were immigrants in 1990. A diverse group, this population includes not only the disadvantaged (one in six lacks a high school education and less than two thirds are proficient in English) but also the highly educated (one in five has a graduate or professional degree; Ong & Hee, 1994, p. 51). On the basis of a 1988 survey, nearly half of the Korean male entrepreneurs had completed college (Fawcett & Gardner, 1994, p. 220). The problems of underemployment, misemployment, and discrimination in the U.S. labor market have turned these educated and professional Asian immigrants toward self-employment. A Korean pharmacist-turned-entrepreneur described the problem of occupational downgrading among Korean pharmacists in southern California: "Most of us find ourselves in a job which is inconsistent with our qualification and experience. We are suffering from starvation wages" (cited in Takaki, 1989, p. 440).

Because of limited capital and skills, Asian American entrepreneurs congregate in highly competitive, marginally profitable, and labor-intensive businesses such as small markets, clothing subcontracting, and restaurants (Ong, 1984, p. 46). According to the 1990 census, one third of the Asian American self-employed are in the retailing sector, with restaurants being the most common operation (Ong & Hee, 1994, pp. 51-52). Asian American ethnic groups differ significantly in the types of businesses they operate—the result of both economic opportunities and ethnic clustering. Korean entrepreneurs are concentrated in the grocery business,[3] dry cleaning services, wholesale and retail sale of Korean imported goods, and American fast food service. Chinese Americans tend to run garment factories, restaurants, and gift shops (Min, 1995, p. 27). Many South Asians, some of them displaced shopowners from Uganda, Kenya, and South Africa, invest in labor-intensive businesses such as hotels and motels. Cambodians have found a niche in the doughnut business—an ideal economic opportunity because it requires little business know-how and almost no English. Today, well over half of the small mom-and-pop doughnut stores and even Winchell's franchises are owned or managed by Cambodian families (Akast, 1993).

Ethnic entrepreneurship is often seen as proof of the benefits of the enterprise system: If people are ambitious and willing to work hard, they can succeed in the United States. In reality, few Asian American business owners manage to achieve upward mobility through entrepreneurship. The majority of the businesses have very low gross earnings and run a high risk of failure. For every successful Asian American businessperson, there are many others who struggle daily to eke out a living. In an analysis of the 1990 census data, Ong and Hee (1994) showed that the median annual income of self-employed Asian Americans is $23,000, which is slightly higher than that of whites ($20,000) (p. 47). But there is a great deal of variation in earnings: A quarter earn $10,400 or less, another quarter earn at least $47,000, and 1% earn over $200,000 (p. 55, n. 17). The chances for business failure appear particularly high for Southeast Asian Americans; for every 20 businesses started by them each month, 18 failed during the first year (May, 1987).

Many Asian American-owned businesses would not be able to survive if it were not for the unpaid or minimally paid labor of spouses, children, relatives, and other oppressed workers. It is unpaid female labor that enables the family store to stay open for as long as 14 hours a day, and on weekends, without having to hire additional workers (Bonacich, Hossain, & Park, 1987, p. 237). According to Ong and Hee (1994), three quarters of Asian American businesses do not have a single outside employee: The typical store is a single-person or a family-run operation (p. 52). In southern California, many Cambodian-owned doughnut shops are open 24 hours a day, with the husband typically baking all night and the wife and teenage children working the counter by day. The profits come directly from the family's labor and from staying open long hours (Akast, 1993; Gold, 1994). According to Ong and Hee (1994), approximately 42% of Asian American business owners work 50 hours or more per week, and 26% work 60 hours or more per week (p. 47). In a study of Chinese Vietnamese entrepreneurs, Steve Gold (1994) noted the hard work and sacrifice of owning a business: "As entrepreneurs, [Chinese Vietnamese] work on slim profit margins, massing family resources and exploiting themselves to maintain marginal or undercapitalized enterprises" (p. 212). Finally, the grandmothers who watch the children while the mothers labor at the family stores form an additional layer of unpaid family labor that also supports these stores (Bonacich et al., 1987, p. 237).

Given the labor-intensive and competitive nature of small businesses, women's participation makes possible the development and viability of family enterprises. Initially, women contribute to capital accumulation by engaging in wage work to provide the additional capital needed to launch a business (Kim & Hurh, 1985). In a study of professional and educated Korean couples in Hawaii, Alice Chai (1987) found that Korean immigrant women resisted both class and domestic oppression by struggling to develop small family businesses where they work in partnership with their husbands. Operating a family business removes them from the racist and sexist labor market and increases their interdependence with their husbands. Women also keep down labor costs by working without pay in the family enterprise (Kim & Hurh, 1988, p. 154).

Because of their crucial contributions to the family enterprise, wives are an economically valuable commodity. A study of Korean immigrants in Elmhurst indicated that "a man cannot even think of establishing his own business without a wife to support and work with" (Park, 1989, p. 144). Corresponding changes in conjugal relationships, however, have been slow and uneven. For instance, the wife's position as co-operator of the family business remains ambiguous. In one sense, she is co-owner of the small business, working for herself and for her family. But in another sense, she is "unpaid family labor," working as an *unpaid* employee of her husband. It is conceivable that for many immigrant women in small business, the latter role predominates. As an example, in a typical Korean-owned business, the husband is the owner-manager and the wife the cashier (Park, 1989, p. 143). In such instances, the husbands can be the women's "most immediate and harshest employers" (Bonacich et al., 1987, p. 237).

Moreover, isolated in and dependent on the ethnic subeconomy, immigrant entrepreneurs are not as influenced by the more flexible gender roles of U.S. middle-class couples and thus seem to be slower than other immigrant groups to discard the rigid gender-role division (Min, 1992). Like housework, managing stores fosters alienation and isolation in that it "affords little time and opportunity for women who run them to develop other skills or to establish close friendships" (Mazumdar, 1989, p. 17). Mrs. Patel, who manages a motel business, describes her typical day:

> I get up at 5:30 in the morning, make breakfast for the family, get the two children ready for school. If there is a guest, I check him in. After the kids are gone, I clean the rooms which have just been vacated, and make all the beds, take out the laundry. . . . In the evening the guests start coming and I check them in. Then I cook. (Thaker, 1982, quoted in Mazumdar, 1989, p. 18)

Note that Mrs. Patel's workday includes both running the family business and executing household responsibilities. In most instances, women's labor in family businesses is defined as an extension of their domestic responsibilities. Kaur, a South Asian immigrant woman who manages the family grocery store, describes the blurred boundaries between home and work:

> I have a desk at home where I do my paperwork. This way I can be home when my daughters get home from school, and when my husband gets home from work I can serve him dinner right away. . . . I bought a stove for the store on which I cook meals for my husband and children during the hours when business is slow at the store. . . . I try to combine my housework with the store work such as grocery shopping. When I go shopping I buy stuff for home and the store. (quoted in Dhaliwal, 1995, p. 80)

The family's construction of Kaur's work as an extension of her domestic responsibilities stabilizes patriarchal ideology in that it reconciles the new gender arrangement (Kaur's participation in the public sphere) with previous gender expectations and ideologies. Some husbands fully expect their wives to work a "double day"—to take care of both their jobs and their homes. Dissatisfied with his wife's performance in the home, a Korean man says, "I understand that women might be too tired to take good care of housework. However, as good and virtuous Korean housewives, they should make more effort at it, with patience" (quoted in Park, 1989, p. 144).

When these small businesses employ co-ethnics, wages are low and working conditions dismal. Ong and Umemoto (1994) listed some of the unfair labor practices endured by workers in ethnic businesses: unpaid wages and unpaid worker's compensation, violation of worker health and safety regulations, and violation of minimum wage laws (p. 100). A Vietnamese entrepreneur defended the use of co-ethnic workers by Chinese Vietnamese entrepreneurs: "We have to understand the employer's position—they need to make a profit. . . . It is good business to pay as little in wages as possible" (cited in Gold, 1994, p. 212).

The exploitation of co-ethnic workers, specifically of women workers, is rampant in the clothing subcontracting business. As discussed earlier, Asian immigrant women make up a significant proportion of garment workers. Asian immigrant men also toil in the garment industry, but mostly as contractors—small-business owners who subcontract from manufacturers to do the cutting and sewing of garments from the manufacturers' designs and textiles. Because they directly employ labor, garment contractors are in a sense labor contractors who mobilize, employ, and control labor for the rest of the industry (Bonacich, 1994). With an investment of as little as $10,000 to $50,000, an entrepreneur can set up a sewing factory—by renting a small work space, purchasing a few used sewing machines, and paying for electricity—and employ 5 to 10 workers (Wong, 1989, pp. 160-161). In a 1989 survey of the Korean Garment Industry Association, Darrel Hess (1990) found that wives, using their previous knowledge of sewing, played a key role in the establishment of contracting firms. Kong Mook Lee of Los Angeles, a Korean pharmacist, explains his decision to invest his money in a garment factory: "The only thing my wife knows is sewing. The only thing I know is pharmacy. Pharmacy is impossible; so sewing is the only way" (cited in Takaki, 1989, p. 440). Lee's example suggests that downward mobility is a common feature of this class, with many educated immigrants falling into the working class.[4]

As middlemen between the manufacturers and the garment workers, these contractors struggle as marginally secure entrepreneurs on the very fringes of the garment industry (Wong, 1983, p. 365). The precarious nature of the business is indicated by the high number of garment factories that close each year (Wong, 1983, p. 370). In New York City, over a quarter of Chinatown garment shops went out of business between 1980 and 1981. Similarly, of the nearly 200 Chinatown garment shops that registered with California's Department of Employment in 1978, 23% were sold or closed by 1982 and another 8% were inactive (Ong, 1984, p. 48). Given the stiff business competition, Asian male contractors have had to exploit the labor of immigrant women to survive. The steady influx of female, limited-English-speaking immigrants puts the sweatshop owner in an extremely powerful position. Because these women have few alternative job opportunities, the owners can virtually dictate the terms of employment: They can pay low wages, ignore overtime work, provide poor working conditions, and fire anyone who is dissatisfied or considered to be a "troublemaker" (Wong, 1983, p. 370). Numerous studies of the Chinatown garment industry conclude that the Chinese women workers are indeed exploited. A 1969 San Francisco Human Rights Commission investigation found that the Chinese women garment workers in Chinatown did not receive overtime pay, vacation, sick leave, or health benefits. A 1982 U.S. Department of Labor report similarly concluded that the Chinese women garment workers in Chinatown were one of the most exploited groups in the New York metropolitan area (Wong, 1983, pp. 365-366). Referring to the unsavory tactics of a co-ethnic contractor, a Chinese garment worker complained that "it's really amazing how the Chinese exploit themselves" (cited in Takaki, 1989, p. 428). It is important to stress that the problem of exploitation is not primarily based on gender or ethnicity but inherent in the organization of the garment industry. Embedded in a larger, hierarchically organized structure, Asian immigrant contractors both victimize the workers they employ and are victimized by those higher up in the hierarchy. The contracting system insulates the industry's principal beneficiaries—the manufacturers, retailers, and bankers—from the grim realities of the sweatshops and the workers' hostility (Bonacich, 1994). Against these more dominant forces, Asian American men and women have, at times, formed a shared sense of ethnic and class solidarity that blunts some of the antagonism in the contractor-worker relationship (Wong, 1983, p. 370; Bonacich, 1994, p. 150).

In sum, the burgeoning Asian immigrant small-business sector is being built, in part, on the racist, patriarchal, and class exploitation of Asian American women. Barred from decent-paying jobs in the general labor market, Asian American women labor long and hard for the benefit of men who are either their husbands or their employers or both—and in many cases, for the benefit of corporate America (Bonacich et al., 1987, p. 238). The ethnic business confers quite different economic and social rewards on men and women (Zhou & Logan, 1989). Whereas men benefit from the unpaid or underpaid female labor, women bear the added burden of the "double workday." Thus, it is critical to recognize that the ethnic economy is both a thriving center and a source of hardship and exploitation for Asian American women.

Conclusion

As a result of the post-1965 influx of Asian immigrants, the contemporary Asian American community is more gender balanced, includes more conjugal families, and fragments more clearly along class lines than in the past. All these changes have important implications for gender and family dynamics within contemporary Asian America. The existing data indicate that changes in relations between Asian American men and women have been slow and uneven. In some cases, greater equality between men and women is the result; in others, it is not. The differences could be attributed to both cultural factors and economic constraints. Along cultural lines, for example, the gender structure in the Philippines is more egalitarian than that of Chinese, Japanese, and Korean societies. As a consequence, women in the Philippines have had and continue to have more or less equal status with men; this gender structure has been reproduced for the most part by Filipino immigrants in the United States. Economic constraints (and opportunities) also structure gender relations within contemporary Asian America. Particularly in the disadvantaged and the self-employed populations, men's dependence on the economic and social resources of women shifts some of the decision-making power to women. This shift has not occurred without friction. Men's loss of status in both public and private arenas has placed severe pressures on the traditional family, leading at times to resentment, spousal abuse, and divorce. For their part, Asian women's ability to restructure the traditional patriarchy system is often constrained by their social-structural location in the dominant society. In the best scenario, responding to the structural barriers in the larger society, both husbands and wives become more interdependent and equal as they are forced to rely on each other, and on the traditional family and immigrant community, for economic security and emotional support. On the other hand, to the extent that the traditional division of labor and male privilege persists, wage work adds to the women's overall workload. The existing research indicates that both of these tendencies exist, though the increased burdens for women are more obvious.

Notes

1. The 1965 Immigration Act specified seven preferences for immigrants: (a) unmarried children over age 21 of U.S. citizens; (b) spouses and unmarried children of permanent residents; (c) professionals, scientists, and artists of "exceptional ability"; (d) married children over age 21 of U.S. citizens; (e) siblings of U.S. citizens; (f) workers, skilled and unskilled, in occupations for which labor was in short supply in the United States; and (g) refugees (Chan, 1991a, p. 146).

2. As gendered and racialized labor, highly educated Asian immigrants are particularly subject to U.S. capital's demotion and manipulation of skilled labor. As such, their "proletarianization" needs to be distinguished from that of white middle-class professionals educated in the United States (Lowe, 1996).

3. By 1983, Koreans dominated the retail produce business in New York City, owning three quarters of the city's 1,200 greengroceries (Takaki, 1989, p. 440).

4. In a study of Taiwan immigrants, Chen (1992) reported that many women who were schoolteachers in Taiwan became knitting workers in the United States because they did not know English. Few of these women will move up again, despite their determination and hard work (p. 249).

CHAPTER 5

Ideological Racism and Cultural Resistance

Constructing Our Own Images

The slit-eyed, bucktooth Jap thrusting his bayonet, thirsty for blood. The inscrutable, wily Chinese detective with his taped eyelids and wispy moustache. The childlike, indolent Filipino houseboy. Always giggling. Bowing and scraping. Eager to please, but untrustworthy. The sexless, hairless Asian male. The servile, oversexed Asian female. The Geisha. The sultry, sarong-clad, South Seas maiden. The serpentine, cunning Dragon Lady. Mysterious and evil, eager to please. Effeminate. Untrustworthy. Yellow Peril. Fortune Cookie Psychic. Savage. Dogeater. Invisible. Mute. Faceless peasants breeding too many children. Gooks. Passive Japanese Americans obediently marching off to "relocation camps" during the Second World War.

Jessica Hagedorn (1993, p. xxii)

Focusing on the material lives of Asian Americans, the earlier chapters explore how racist and gendered immigration policies and labor conditions have worked in tandem to keep Asian Americans in an assigned, subordinate place. But as is evident from the stereotypes listed above, besides structural discrimination, Asian American men and women have been subject to ideological assaults. Focusing on the ideological dimension of Asian American oppression, this chapter examines the cultural symbols—or what Patricia Hill Collins (1991) called "controlling images"

AUTHOR'S NOTE: The excerpt from Cao Tan's poem, "Tomorrow I Will Be Home," appeared in *War and exile: A Vietnamese anthology*, edited by N. N. Bich, 1989, Springfield, VA: Vietnam PEN Abroad.

(pp. 67-68)—generated by the dominant group to help justify the economic exploitation and social oppression of Asian American men and women over time. Writing on the objectification of black women, Collins (1991) observed that the exercise of political-economic domination by racial elites "always involves attempts to objectify the subordinate group" (p. 69). Transmitted through cultural institutions owned, controlled, or supported by various elites, these "controlling images" naturalize racism, sexism, and poverty by branding subordinate groups as alternatively inferior, threatening, or praiseworthy. These controlling images form part of a larger system of what Donald G. Baker (1983) referred to as "psychosocial dominance" (p. 37). Along with the threat and occasional use of violence, the psychosocial form of control conditions the subject minority to become the stereotype, to "live it, talk it, embrace it, measure group and individual worth in its terms, and believe it" (Chin & Chan, 1972, pp. 66-67). In so doing, minority members reject their own individual and group identity and accept in its stead "a white supremacist complex that establishes the primacy of Euro-American cultural practices and social institutions" (Hamamoto, 1994, p. 2). But the objectification of Asian Americans as the exotic and inferior "other" has never been absolute. Asian Americans have always, but particularly since the 1960s, resisted race, class, and gender exploitation not only through political and economic struggles but also through cultural activism. This chapter surveys the range of oppositional projects in which Asian American cultural workers have engaged to deconstruct the conceptual apparatus of the dominant group and to defend Asian American manhood and womanhood. My goal is to understand how the internalization and renunciation of these stereotypes have shaped sexual and gender politics within Asian America. In particular, I explore the conflicting politics of gender between Asian American men and women as they negotiate the difficult terrain of cultural nationalism—the construction of an antiassimilationist, native Asian American subject—and gender identities. Unlike the previous chapters, which rely on historical, sociological, and anthropological works, this chapter draws heavily from the fields of cultural studies and literary criticism.

Yellow Peril, Charlie Chan, and Suzie Wong

A central aspect of racial exploitation centers on defining people of color as "the other" (Said, 1979). The social construction of Asian American "otherness"—through such controlling images as the Yellow

Peril, the model minority, the Dragon Lady, and the China Doll—is "the precondition for their cultural marginalization, political impotence, and psychic alienation from mainstream American society" (Hamamoto, 1994, p. 5). As indicated by these stereotypes, representations of gender and sexuality figure strongly in the articulation of racism. These racist stereotypes collapse gender and sexuality: Asian men have been constructed as hypermasculine, in the image of the "Yellow Peril," but also as effeminate, in the image of the "model minority," and Asian women have been depicted as superfeminine, in the image of the "China Doll," but also as castrating, in the image of the "Dragon Lady" (Mullings, 1994, pp. 279-280; Okihiro, 1995). As Mary Ann Doane (1991) suggested, sexuality is "indissociable from the effects of polarization and differentiation, often linking them to structures of power and domination" (p. 217). In the Asian American case, the gendering of ethnicity—the process whereby white ideology assigns selected gender characteristics to various ethnic "others"—cast Asian American men and women as simultaneously masculine and feminine but also as neither masculine nor feminine. On the one hand, as part of the Yellow Peril, Asian American men and women have been depicted as a *masculine* threat that needs to be contained. On the other hand, both sexes have been skewed toward the female side: an indication of the group's marginalization in U.S. society and its role as the compliant "model minority" in contemporary U.S. cultural ideology. Although an apparent disjunction, both the feminization and masculinization of Asian men and women exist to define and confirm the white man's superiority (Kim, 1990).

The Yellow Peril

In the United States, Asia and America—East and West—are viewed as mutually exclusive binaries (Kim, 1993, p. viii). Within this exclusive binary system, Asian Americans, even as citizens, are designated Asians, not Americans. Characterizing Asian Americans as "permanent houseguests in the house of America," Sau-Ling Cynthia Wong (1993) stated that "Asian Americans are put in the niche of the 'unassimilable alien': . . . they are alleged to be self-disqualified from full American membership by materialistic motives, questionable political allegiance, and, above all, outlandish, overripe, 'Oriental' cultures" (p. 6). Sonia Shah (1994) defined this form of "cultural discrimination" as a "peculiar blend of cultural and sexist oppression based on our accents, our clothes, our foods, our values and our commitments" (p. 182). This cultural discrimination brands Asians as perpetual foreigners and thus perpetuates the notion of their alleged racial unassimilability. For example, although Japanese Americans have lived in the United States since the turn of the century, many television programs, such as *Happy Days* (1974-1984) and *Gung Ho* (1986-1987), have continued to portray them as newly arrived foreigners (Hamamoto, 1994, p. 13).

As the unassimilable alien, Asian Americans embody for many other Americans the "Yellow Peril"—the threat that Asians will one day unite and conquer the world. This threat includes military invasion and foreign trade from Asia, competition to white labor from Asian labor, the alleged moral degeneracy of Asian people, and potential miscegenation between whites and Asians (Wu, 1982, p. 1). Between 1850 and 1940, U.S. popular media consistently portrayed Asian men as a military threat to the security and welfare of the United States *and* as a sexual danger to innocent white women (Wu, 1982). In numerous dime novels, movies, and comic strips, Asians appeared as feral, rat-faced men lusting after virginal white women. Arguing for racial purity, these popular media depicted Asian-white sexual union as "at best, a form of beastly sodomy, and, at worst, a Satanic marriage" (Hoppenstand, 1983, p. 174). In these popular depictions, the white man was the desirable sexual partner and the hero who rescued the white woman from "a fate worse than death" (Hoppenstand, 1983, pp. 174-175). By the mid-1880s, hundreds of garishly illustrated and garishly written dime novels were being disseminated among a wide audience, sporting such sensational titles as *The Bradys and the Yellow Crooks*, *The Chase for the Chinese Diamonds*, *The Opium Den Detective*, and *The Stranglers of New York*. As portrayed in these dime novels, the Yellow Peril was the Chinatown district of a big city "in which decent, honest white folk never ventured" (Hoppenstand, 1983, p. 177).

In 20th-century U.S. popular media, the Japanese joined the Chinese as a perceived threat to Europe and the United States (Wu, 1982, p. 2). In 1916, William Randolph Hearst produced and distributed *Petria*, a movie about a group of fanatical Japanese who invade the United States and attempt to rape a white woman (Quinsaat, 1976, p. 265). After the Japanese bombing of Pearl Harbor on December 7, 1941, the entire Yellow Peril stereotype became incorporated in the nation's war propaganda, quickly whipping white Americans into a war fever. Along with the print media, Hollywood cranked up its anti-Japanese propaganda and produced dozens of war films that centered on the Japanese menace. The fiction of the Yellow Peril stereotype became intertwined with the fact of the United States' war with Japan, and the two became one in the mind-set of the American public (Hoppenstand, 1983, pp. 182-183). It was fear of the Yellow Peril—fear of the rise of nonwhite people and their contestation of white supremacy—that led to the declaration of martial law in Hawaii on December 7, 1941, and to the internment of over 110,000 Japanese on the mainland in concentration camps (Okihiro, 1994, p. 137). In subsequent decades, reflecting changing geopolitical concerns, U.S. popular media featured a host of new yellow peril stereotypes. During the 1950s Cold War years, in television programs as well as in movies, the Communist Chinese evildoers replaced the Japanese monster; during the Vietnam war of the 1970s, the Vietnamese Communists emerged as the new Oriental villains.

Today, Yellow Perilism takes the forms of the greedy, calculating, and clever Japanese businessman aggressively buying up U.S. real estate and cultural institutions *and* the superachieving but nonassimilating Asian Americans (Hagedorn, 1993, p. xxii). In a time of rising economic powers in Asia, declining economic opportunities in the United States, and growing diversity among America's people, this new Yellow Perilism—the depiction of Asia and Asian Americans as economic and cultural threats to mainstream United States—supplies white Americans with a united identity and provides ideological justification for U.S. isolationist policy toward Asia, increasing restrictions against Asian (and Latino) immigration,[1] and the invisible institutional racism and visible violence against Asians in the United States (Okihiro, 1994, pp. 138-139).

The Racial Construction of Asian American Manhood

Like other men of color, Asian American men have been excluded from white-based cultural notions of the masculine. Whereas white men are depicted both as virile and as protectors of women, Asian men have been characterized both as asexual *and* as threats to white women. It is important to note the historical contexts of these seemingly divergent representations of Asian American manhood. The racist depictions of Asian men as "lascivious and predatory" were especially pronounced during the nativist movement against Asians at the turn of the century (Frankenberg, 1993, pp. 75-76). The exclusion of Asian women from the United States and the subsequent establishment of bachelor societies eventually reversed the construction of Asian masculinity from "hypersexual" to "asexual" and even "homosexual." The contemporary model-minority stereotype further emasculates Asian American men as passive and malleable. Disseminated and perpetuated through the popular media, these stereotypes of the emasculated Asian male construct a reality in which social and economic discrimination against these men appears defensible. As an example, the desexualization of Asian men naturalized their inability to establish conjugal families in pre-World War II United States. Gliding over race-based exclusion laws that banned the immigration of most Asian women and antimiscegenation laws that prohibited men of color from marrying white women, these dual images of the eunuch and the rapist attributed the "womanless households" characteristic of pre-war Asian America to Asian men's lack of sexual prowess and desirability.

A popular controlling image applied to Asian American men is that of the sinister Oriental—a brilliant, powerful villain who plots the destruction of Western civilization. Personified by the movie character of Dr. Fu Manchu, this Oriental mastermind combines Western science with Eastern magic and commands an army of devoted assassins (Hoppenstand, 1983, p. 178). Though ruthless, Fu Manchu lacks masculine heterosexual prowess (Wang, 1988, p. 19), thus privileging heterosexuality. Frank Chin and Jeffrey Chan (1972), in a critique of the desexualization of Asian men in Western culture, described how the Fu Manchu character undermines Chinese American virility:

> Dr. Fu, a man wearing a long dress, batting his eyelashes, surrounded by muscular black servants in loin cloths, and with his habit of caressingly touching white men on the leg, wrist, and face with his long fingernails is not so much a threat as he is a frivolous offense to white manhood. (p. 60)

In another critique that glorifies male aggression, Frank Chin (1972) contrasted the neuterlike characteristics assigned to Asian men to the sexually aggressive images associated with other men of color: "Unlike the white stereotype of the evil black stud, Indian rapist, Mexican macho, the evil of the evil Dr. Fu Manchu was not sexual, but homosexual" (p. 66). However, Chin failed to note that as a homosexual, Dr. Fu (and by extension, Asian men) threatens and offends white masculinity—and therefore needs to be contained ideologically and destroyed physically.[2]

Whereas the evil Oriental stereotype marks Asian American men as the white man's enemy, the stereotype of the sexless Asian sidekick—Charlie Chan, the Chinese laundryman, the Filipino houseboy—depicts Asian men as devoted and impotent, eager to please. William Wu (1982) reported that the Chinese servant "is the most important single image of the Chinese immigrants" in American fiction about Chinese Americans between 1850 and 1940 (p. 60). More recently, such diverse television programs as *Bachelor Father* (1957-1962), *Bonanza* (1959-1973), *Star Trek* (1966-1969), and *Falcon Crest* (1981-1990) all featured the stock Chinese bachelor domestic who dispenses sage advice to his superiors in addition to performing traditional female functions within the household (Hamamoto, 1994, p. 7). By trapping Chinese men (and by extension, Asian men) in the stereotypical "feminine" tasks of serving white men, American society erases the figure of the Asian "masculine" plantation worker in Hawaii or railroad construction worker in the western United States, thus perpetuating the myth of the androgynous and effeminate Asian man (Goellnicht, 1992, p. 198). This feminization, in turn, confines Asian immigrant men to the segment of the labor force that performs women's work.

The motion picture industry has been key in the construction of Asian men as sexual deviants. In a study of Asians in the U.S. motion pictures, Eugene Franklin Wong (1978) maintained that the movie industry filmically castrates Asian males to magnify the superior sexual status of white males (p. 27). As on-screen sexual rivals of whites, Asian males are neutralized, unable to sexually engage Asian women and prohibited from sexually engaging white women. By saving the white woman from sexual contact with the racial "other," the motion picture industry protects the Anglo-American, bourgeois male establishment from any challenges to its hegemony (Marchetti, 1993, p. 218). At the other extreme, the industry has exploited one of the most potent aspects of the Yellow Peril discourses—the sexual danger of contact between the races—by concocting a sexually threatening portrayal of the licentious and aggressive Yellow Man lusting after the White Woman (Marchetti, 1993, p. 3). Heedful of the larger society's taboos against Asian male-white female sexual union, white male actors donning "yellowface"—instead of Asian male actors—are used in these "love scenes." Nevertheless, the message of the perverse and animalistic Asian male attacking helpless white women is clear (Wong, 1978). Though depicting sexual aggression, this image of the rapist, like that of the eunuch, casts Asian men as sexually undesirable. As Wong (1978) succinctly stated, in Asian male-white female relations, "There can be rape, but there cannot be romance" (p. 25). Thus, Asian males yield to the sexual superiority of the white males who are permitted filmically to maintain their sexual dominance over both white women and women of color. A young Vietnamese American man describes the damaging effect of these stereotypes on his self-image:

Every day I was forced to look into a mirror created by white society and its media. As a young Asian man, I shrank before white eyes. I wasn't tall, I wasn't fair, I wasn't muscular, and so on. Combine that with the enormous insecurities any pubescent teenager feels, and I have no difficulty in knowing now why I felt naked before a mass of white people. (Nguyen, 1990, p. 23)

White cultural and institutional racism against Asian males is also reflected in the motion picture industry's preoccupation with the death of Asians—a filmic solution to the threats of the Yellow Peril. In a perceptive analysis of Hollywood's view of Asians in films made from the 1930s to the 1960s, Tom Engelhardt (1976) described how Asians, like Native Americans, are seen by the movie industry as inhuman invaders, ripe for extermination. He argued that the theme of the nonhumanness of Asians prepares the audience to accept, without flinching, "the levelling and near-obliteration of three Asian areas in the course of three decades" (Engelhardt, 1976, p. 273). The industry's death theme, though applying to all Asians, is mainly focused on Asian males, with Asian females reserved for sexual purposes (Wong, 1978, p. 35). Especially in war films, Asian males, however advantageous their initial position, inevitably perish at the hands of the superior white males (Wong, 1978, p. 34).

The Racial Construction of
Asian American Womanhood

Like Asian men, Asian women have been reduced to one-dimensional caricatures in Western representation. The condensation of Asian women's multiple differences into gross character types—mysterious, feminine, and nonwhite—obscures the social injustice of racial, class, and gender oppression (Marchetti, 1993, p. 71). Both Western film and literature promote dichotomous stereotypes of the Asian woman: Either she is the cunning Dragon Lady or the servile Lotus Blossom Baby (Tong, 1994, p. 197). Though connoting two extremes, these stereotypes are interrelated: Both eroticize Asian women as exotic "others"—sensuous, promiscuous, but untrustworthy. Whereas American popular culture denies "manhood" to Asian men, it endows Asian women with an excess of "womanhood," sexualizing them but also impugning their sexuality. In this process, both sexism and racism have been blended together to produce the sexualization of white racism (Wong, 1978, p. 260). Linking the controlling images of Asian men and women, Elaine Kim (1990) suggested that Asian women are portrayed as sexual for the same reason that men are asexual: "Both exist to define the white man's virility and the white man's superiority" (p. 70).

As the racialized exotic "others," Asian American women do not fit the white-constructed notions of the feminine. Whereas white women have been depicted as chaste and dependable, Asian women have been represented as promiscuous and untrustworthy. In a mirror image of the evil Fu Manchu, the Asian woman was portrayed as the castrating Dragon Lady who, while puffing on her foot-long cigarette holder, could poison a man as easily as she could seduce him. "With her talon-like six-inch fingernails, her skin-tight satin dress slit to the thigh," the Dragon Lady is desirable, deceitful, and dangerous (Ling, 1990, p. 11). In the 1924 film *The Thief of Baghdad*, Anna May Wong, a pioneer Chinese American actress, played a handmaid who employed treachery to help an evil Mongol prince attempt to win the hand of the Princess of Baghdad (Tajima, 1989, p. 309). In so doing, Wong unwittingly popularized a common Dragon Lady social type: treacherous women who are partners in crime with men of their own kind. The publication of *Daughter of Fu Manchu* (1931) firmly entrenched the Dragon Lady image in white consciousness. Carrying on her father's work as the champion of Asian hegemony over the white race, Fah Lo Sue exhibited, in the words of American studies scholar William F. Wu, "exotic sensuality, sexual availability to a white man, and a treacherous nature" (cited in Tong, 1994, p. 197). A few years later, in 1934, Milton Caniff inserted into his adventure comic strip *Terry and the Pirates* another version of the Dragon Lady who "combines all the best features of past moustache twirlers with the lure of the handsome wench" (Hoppenstand, 1983, p. 178). As such, Caniff's Dragon Lady fuses the image of the evil male Oriental mastermind with that of the Oriental prostitute first introduced some 50 years earlier in the dime novels.

At the opposite end of the spectrum is the Lotus Blossom stereotype, reincarnated throughout the years as the China Doll, the Geisha Girl, the War Bride, or the Vietnamese prostitute—many of whom are the spoils of the last three wars fought in Asia (Tajima, 1989, p. 309). Demure, diminutive, and deferential, the Lotus Blossom Baby is "modest, tittering behind her delicate ivory hand, eyes downcast, always walking ten steps behind her man, and, best of all, devot[ing] body and soul to serving him" (Ling, 1990, p. 11). Interchangeable in appearance and name, these women have no voice; their "nonlanguage" includes uninterpretable chattering, pidgin English, giggling, or silence (Tajima, 1989). These stereotypes of Asian women as submissive and dainty sex objects not only have impeded women's economic mobility but also have fostered an enormous demand for X-rated films and pornographic materials featuring Asian women in bondage, for "Oriental" bathhouse workers in U.S. cities, and for Asian mail-order brides (Kim, 1984, p. 64).

Sexism, Racism, and Love

The racialization of Asian manhood and womanhood upholds white masculine hegemony. Cast as sexually available, Asian women become yet another possession of the white man. In motion pictures and network television programs, interracial sexuality, though rare, occurs principally between a white male and an Asian female. A combination of sexism and racism makes this form of miscegenation more acceptable: Race mixing between an Asian male and a white female would upset not only racial taboos but those that attend patriarchal authority as well (Hamamoto, 1994, p. 39). Whereas Asian men are depicted as either the threatening rapist or the impotent eunuch, white men are endowed with the masculine attributes with which to sexually attract the Asian woman. Such popular television shows as *Gunsmoke* (1955-1975) and *How the West Was Won* (1978-1979) clearly articulate the theme of Asian female sexual possession by the white male. In these shows, only white males have the prerogative to cross racial boundaries and to choose freely from among women of color as sex partners. Within a system of racial and gender oppression, the sexual possession of women and men of color by white men becomes yet another means of enforcing unequal power relations (Hamamoto, 1994, p. 46).

The preference for white male-Asian female is also prevalent in contemporary television news broadcasting, most recently in the 1993-1995 pairing of Dan Rather and Connie Chung as coanchors of the *CBS Evening News*. Today, virtually every major metropolitan market across the United States has at least one Asian American female newscaster (Hamamoto, 1994, p. 245). While female Asian American anchorpersons—Connie Chung, Tritia Toyota, Wendy Tokuda, and Emerald Yeh—are popular television news figures, there is a nearly total absence of Asian American men. Critics argue that this is so because the white male hiring establishment, and presumably the larger American public, feels more comfortable (i.e., less threatened) seeing a white male sitting next to a minority female at the anchor desk than the reverse. Stephen Tschida of WDBJ-TV (Roanoke, Virginia), one of only a handful of male Asian American television news anchors, was informed early in his career that he did not have the proper "look" to qualify for the anchorperson position. Other male broadcast news veterans have reported being passed over for younger, more beauteous, female Asian Americans (Hamamoto, 1994, p. 245). This gender imbalance sustains the construction of Asian American women as more successful, assimilated, attractive, and desirable than their male counterparts.

To win the love of white men, Asian women must reject not only Asian men but their entire culture. Many Hollywood narratives featuring romances between Anglo American men and Asian women follow the popular Pocahontas mythos: The Asian woman, out of devotion for her white American lover, betrays her own people and commits herself to the dominant white culture by dying, longing for, or going to live with her white husband in his country. For example, in the various versions of *Miss Saigon*, the contemporary version of *Madame Butterfly*, the tragic Vietnamese prostitute eternally longs for the white boy soldier who has long abandoned her and their son (Hagedorn, 1993, p. xxii). These tales of interracial romance inevitably have a tragic ending. The Asian partner usually dies, thus providing a cinematic resolution to the moral lapse of the Westerner. The Pocahontas paradigm can be read as a narrative of salvation; the Asian woman is saved either spiritually or morally from the excesses of her own culture, just as she physically saves her Western lover from the moral degeneracy of her own people (Marchetti, 1993, p. 218). For Asian women, who are marginalized not only by gender but also by class, race, or ethnicity, the interracial romance narratives promise "the American Dream of abundance, protection, individual choice, and freedom from the strictures of a traditional society in the paternalistic name of heterosexual romance" (Marchetti, 1993, p. 91). These narratives also carry a covert political message, legitimizing a masculinized Anglo American rule over a submissive, feminized Asia. The motion picture *China Gate* (1957) by Samuel Fuller and the network television program *The Lady From Yesterday* (1985), for example, promote an image of Vietnam that legitimizes American rule. Seduced by images of U.S. abundance, a feminized Vietnam sacrifices herself for the possibility of future incorporation into America, the land of individual freedom and economic opportunities. Thus, the interracial tales function not only as a romantic defense of traditional female roles within the patriarchy but also as a political justification of American hegemony in Asia (Marchetti, 1993, p. 108).

Fetishized as the embodiment of perfect womanhood and genuine exotic femininity, Asian women are pitted against their more modern, emancipated Western sisters (Tajima, 1989). In two popular motion pictures, *Love Is a Many-Splendored Thing* (1955) and *The World of Suzie Wong* (1960), the white women remain independent and potentially threatening, whereas both Suyin and Suzie give up their independence in the name of love. Thus, the white female characters are cast as calculating, suffocating, and thoroughly undesirable, whereas the Asian female characters are depicted as truly "feminine"—passive, subservient, dependent, and domestic. Implicitly, these films warn white women to embrace the socially constructed passive Asian beauty as the feminine ideal if they want to attract and keep a man. In pitting white women against Asian women, Hollywood affirms white male identity against the threat of emerging feminism and the concomitant changes in gender relations (Marchetti, 1993, pp. 115-116). As Robyn Wiegman (1991) observed, the absorption of women of color into gender categories traditionally reserved for white women is "part of a broader program of hegemonic recuperation, a program that has at its main focus the reconstruction of white masculine power" (p. 320). It is also important to note that as the racialized exotic "other," Asian women do not replace but merely substitute for white women, and thus will be readily dismissed once the "real" mistress returns.

The controlling images of Asian men and Asian women, exaggerated out of all proportion in Western representation, have created resentment and tension between Asian American men and women. Given this cultural milieu, many American-born Asians do not think of other Asians in sexual terms (Fung, 1994, p. 163). In particular, due to the persistent desexualization of the Asian male, many Asian females do not perceive their ethnic counterparts as desirable marriage partners (Hamamoto, 1992, p. 42). In so doing, these women unwittingly enforce the Eurocentric gender ideology that objectifies both sexes and racializes all Asians (see Collins, 1990, pp. 185-186). In a column to *Asian Week*, a weekly Asian American newspaper, Daniel Yoon (1993) reported that at a recent dinner discussion hosted by the Asian American Students Association at his college, the Asian American women in the room proceeded, one after another, to describe how "Asian American men were too passive, too weak, too boring, too traditional, too abusive, too domineering, too ugly, too greasy, too short, too . . . Asian. Several described how they preferred white men, and how they never had and never would date an Asian man" (p. 16). Partly as a result of the racist constructions of Asian American womanhood and manhood and their acceptance by Asian Americans, intermarriage patterns are high, with Asian American women intermarrying at a much higher rate than Asian

American men.[3] Moreover, Asian women involved in intermarriage have usually married white partners (Agbayani-Siewert & Revilla, 1995, p. 156; Min, 1995, p. 22; Nishi, 1995, p. 128). In part, these intermarriage patterns reflect the sexualization of white racism that constructs white men as the most desirable sexual partners, frowns on Asian male-white women relations, and fetishizes Asian women as the embodiment of perfect womanhood. Viewed in this light, the high rate of outmarriage for Asian American women is the "material outcome of an interlocking system of sexism and racism" (Hamamoto, 1992, p. 42).[4]

Cultural Resistance:
Reconstructing Our Own Images

"One day/I going to write/about you," wrote Lois-Ann Yamanaka (1993) in "Empty Heart" (p. 548). And Asian Americans did write—"to inscribe our faces on the blank pages and screens of America's hegemonic culture" (Kim, 1993, p. xii). As a result, Asian Americans' objectification as the exotic aliens who are different from, and other than, Euro-Americans has never been absolute. Within the confines of race, class, and gender oppression, Asian Americans have maintained independent self-definitions, challenging controlling images and replacing them with Asian American standpoints. The civil rights and ethnic studies movements of the late 1960s were training grounds for Asian American cultural workers and the development of oppositional projects. Grounded in the U.S. black power movement and in anticolonial struggles of Third World countries, Asian American antihegemonic projects have been unified by a common goal of articulating cultural resistance. Given the historical distortions and misrepresentations of Asian Americans in mainstream media, most cultural projects produced by Asian American men and women perform the important tasks of correcting histories, shaping legacies, creating new cultures, constructing a politics of resistance, and opening spaces for the forcibly excluded (Kim, 1993, p. xiii; Fung, 1994, p. 165).

Fighting the exoticization of Asian Americans has been central in the ongoing work of cultural resistance. As discussed above, Asian Americans, however rooted in this country, are represented as recent transplants from Asia or as bearers of an exotic culture. The Chinese American playwright Frank Chin noted that New York critics of his play *Chickencoop Chinaman* complained in the early 1970s that his characters did not speak, dress, or act "like Orientals" (Kim, 1982, p. xv).

Similarly, a reviewer described Maxine Hong Kingston's *The Woman Warrior* as a tale of "East meets West" and praised the book for its "myths rich and varied as Chinese brocade"—even though *The Woman Warrior* is deliberately anti-exotic and anti-nostalgic (quoted in Kim, 1982, p. xvi). In both of these examples, the qualifier *American* has been blithely excised from the term *Asian American*.

Asian American cultural workers simply do not accept the exotic, one-dimensional caricatures of themselves in U.S. mass media. In the preface of *Aiiieeeee!*, a landmark collection of Asian American writers (in this case, Chinese, Japanese, and Filipinos), published in the mid-1970s, the editors announced that the anthology, and the title *Aiiieeeee!* itself, challenged the exoticization of Asian Americans:

> The pushers of white American culture . . . pictured the yellow man as something that when wounded, sad, angry, or swearing, or wondering whined, shouted, or screamed "aiiieeeee!" Asian America, so long ignored and forcibly excluded from creative participation in American culture, is wounded, sad, angry, swearing, and wondering, and this is his AIIIEEEEE!!! It is more than a whine, shout, or scream. It is fifty years of our whole voice. (Chan et al., 1974, p. xii)

The publication of *Aiiieeeee!* gave Asian American writers visibility and credibility and sparked other oppositional projects. Jessica Hagedorn, a Filipina American writer, described the legacy of *Aiiieeeee!*: "We could not be ignored; suddenly, we were no longer silent. Like other writers of color in America, we were beginning to challenge the long-cherished concepts of a xenophobic literary canon dominated by white heterosexual males" (Hagedorn, 1993, p. xviii). Inspired by *Aiiieeeee!* and by other "irreverent and blasphemous" American writers, Hagedorn created an anthology of contemporary Asian American fiction in 1993—"a book I wanted to read but had never been available to me" (Hagedorn, 1993, p. xxx). In the tradition of *Aiiieeeee!*, the title of Hagedorn's anthology, *Charlie Chan Is Dead*, is vigorously political, defying and stamping out the vestiges of a "fake 'Asian' pop icon" (Hagedorn, 1993, p. xxi). In the anthology's preface, Elaine Kim (1993) contested the homogenization of Asian Americans by juxtaposing the one-dimensional Charlie Chan to the many ways of being Asian American in contemporary United States:

> Charlie Chan is dead, never to be revived. Gone for good his yellowface asexual bulk, his fortune-cookie English, his stereotypical Orientalist version of "the [Confucian] Chinese family," challenged by an array of

characters, some hip and articulate, some brooding and sexy, some insolent and others innocent, but all as unexpected as a Korean American who writes in French, a Chinese-Panamanian-German who longs too late to know her father, a mean Japanese American grandmother, a Chinese American flam-dive, or a teenaged Filipino American male prostitute. Instead of "model minorities," we find human beings with rich and complex pasts and brave, often flamboyant dreams of the future. (p. xiii)

Taking up this theme, Wayne Chang's commercial film *Chan Is Missing* (1981) offers a range of Chinatown characters who indirectly convey the message that Chinese Americans, like other Americans, are heterogeneous (Chan, 1994, p. 530). Portraying Asian Americans in all our contradictions and complexities—as exiled, assimilated, rebellious, noble—Asian American cultural projects reveal heterogeneity rather than "producing regulating ideas of cultural unity or integration" (Lowe, 1994, p. 53). In so doing, these projects destabilize the dominant racist discourse that constructs Asians as a homogeneous group who are "all alike" and readily conform to "types" such as the Yellow Peril, the Oriental mastermind, and the sexy Suzie Wong (Lowe, 1991).

Asian American cultural projects also deconstruct the myth of the benevolent United States promised to women and men from Asia. Carlos Bulosan's *America Is in the Heart* (1943/1973), one of the core works of Asian American literature, challenges the narrative of the United States as the land of opportunity. Seduced by the promise of individual freedom through education, the protagonist Carlos discovers that as a Filipino immigrant in the United States, he is denied access to formal schooling. This disjunction between the promise of education and the unequal access of different racial and economic groups to that education—reinforced by Carlos's observations of the exploitation, marginality, and violence suffered by his compatriots in the United States—challenges his faith in the promise of U.S. democracy and abundance (Lowe, 1994, p. 56). John Okada's *No-No Boy* (1957) is another searing indictment of U.S. racist hysteria. In this portrayal of the aftermath of the internment of Japanese Americans during World War II, the protagonist, Ichiro, angrily refuses to adjust to his postinternment and postimprisonment circumstances, thus dramatizing the Asian American subject's refusal to accept the subordinating terms of assimilation (Lowe, 1994, p. 59). In the following excerpt from the poem by Cao Tan, "Tomorrow I Will Be Home," a Vietnamese refugee describes the emasculating effect of U.S. society:

Tomorrow I will be home and someone will ask

What have you learned in the States?

If you want to give me a broom

I'll tell you, I am a first class janitor.

I wash dishes much faster than the best housewife

And do a vacuum job better than any child

Every day I run like a madman in my brand new car

Every night I bury my head in my pillow and cry. . . .

Bich (1989)

To reject the myth of a benevolent United States is also to refute ideological racism: the justification of inequalities through a set of controlling images that attribute physical and intellectual traits to racially defined groups (Hamamoto, 1994, p. 3). In the 1980 autobiographical fiction *China Men*, Maxine Hong Kingston smashed the controlling image of the emasculated Asian man by foregrounding the legalized racism that turned immigrant Chinese "men" into "women" at the turn of the century. In his search for the Gold Mountain, the novel's male protagonist Tang Ao finds instead the Land of Women, where he is caught and transformed into an Oriental courtesan. Because Kingston reveals at the end of the legend that the Land of Women was in North America, readers familiar with Chinese American history will readily see that "the ignominy suffered by Tang Ao in a foreign land symbolizes the emasculation of Chinamen by the dominant culture" (Cheung, 1990, p. 240). Later in the novel, the father's failure as a provider—his emasculation—inverts the sexual roles in the family. His silence and impotent rage deepen as his wife takes on active power in the family and assumes the "masculine" traits of aggressiveness and authority. As a means of releasing his sense of frustration and powerlessness in racist America, the father lapses into silence, screams "wordless male screams in his sleep," and spouts furious misogynistic curses that frighten his daughter (Sledge, 1980, p. 10). The author/narrator Maxine traces her father's abusive behavior back to his feeling of emasculation in America: "We knew that it was to feed us you had to endure demons and physical labor" (cited in Goellnicht, 1992, p. 201). Similarly, in Louis Chu's 1961 novel *Eat a Bowl of Tea*, the protagonist's sexual impotence represents the social powerlessness of generations of Chinatown bachelors prevented by discriminatory laws and policies from establishing a traditional family life (Kim, 1982, p. xviii).

More recently, Steven Okazaki's film *American Sons* (1995)[5] tells the stories of four Asian American men who reveal how incidents of prejudice and bigotry shaped their identity and affected the way they perceived themselves and society. About his film, Okazaki (1995) explained, "Prejudice, bigotry, and violence twist and demean individual lives. *American Sons* looks at difficult issues, such as hate violence, in order to show this intimate and disturbing examination of the deep psychological damage that racism causes over generations" (n.p.). Asian American men's increasing involvement in hip-hop—a highly masculinized cultural form and a distinctly American phenomenon—is yet another contemporary denouncement of the stereotype of themselves as "effeminate, nerdy, asocial foreigners" (Choe, 1996). By exposing the role of the larger society in the emasculation and oppression of Asian men, Kingston, Chu, and Okazaki invalidated the naturalization and normalization of Asian men's asexuality in U.S. popular culture.

Finally, Asian American cultural workers reject the narrative of salvation: the myth that Asian women (and a feminized Asia) are saved, through sexual relations with white men (and a masculinized United States), from the excesses of their own culture. Instead, they underscore the considerable potential for abuse in these inherently unequal relationships. Writing in Vietnamese, transplanted Vietnamese writer Tran Dieu Hang described the gloomy existence of Vietnamese women in sexist and racist U.S. society—an accursed land that singles out women, especially immigrant women, for oppression and violence. Her short story "Roi Ngay Van Moi" ("There Will Come New Days"; 1986) depicts the brutal rape of a young refugee woman by her American sponsor despite her tearful pleas in limited English (Tran, 1993, pp. 72-73). Marianne Villanueva's short story "Opportunity" (1991) also calls attention to the sexualization and racialization of Asian women. As the protagonist Nina, a "mail-order bride" from the Philippines, enters the hotel lobby to meet her American fiance, the bellboys snicker and whisper *puta*, whore: a reminder that U.S. economic and cultural colonization of the Philippines always forms the backdrop to any relations between Filipinos and Americans (Wong, 1993, p. 53). Characterizing Filipino American literature as a "literature of exile," Oscar Campomanes (1992) underscored the legacy of U.S. colonization of the Philippines: "The signifiers 'Filipinos' and 'Philippines' evoke colonialist meanings and cultural redactions which possess inordinate power to shape the fates of the writers and of Filipino peoples everywhere" (p. 52). Theresa Hak Kyung Cha's *Dictee* (1982), a Korean American text, likewise challenges the myth of U.S. benevolence in Asia by tracing the impact of colonial and imperial damage and dislocation on the Korean subject (Lowe, 1994, p. 61). As Sau-Ling Cynthia Wong (1993) suggested, "To the extent that most typical cases of Asian immigration to the United States stem from an imbalance of resources writ large in the world economy, it holds in itself the seed of exploitation" (p. 53).

Controlling Images, Gender, and Cultural Nationalism

Cultural nationalism has been crucial in Asian Americans' struggles for self-determination. Emerging in the early 1970s, this unitary Asian American identity was primarily racial, male, and heterosexual. Asian American literature produced in those years highlighted Chinese and Japanese American male perspectives, obscuring gender and other intercommunity differences (Kim, 1993). Asian American male writers, concerned with recuperating their identities as men and as Americans, objectified both white and Asian women in their writings (Kim, 1990, p. 70). In a controversial essay entitled "Racist Love," Frank Chin and Jeffrey Paul Chan (1972) pointed to the stereotype of the emasculated Asian American man:

> The white stereotype of Asian is unique in that it is the only racial stereotype completely devoid of manhood. Our nobility is that of an efficient housewife. At our worst we are contemptible because we are womanly, effeminate, devoid of all the traditionally masculine qualities of originality, daring, physical courage, creativity. (p. 68)

In taking whites to task for their racist debasement of Asian American men, however, Chin and Chan succumbed to the influence of Eurocentric gender ideology, particularly its emphasis on oppositional dichotomous sex roles (Collins, 1991, p. 184). In a critique of "Racist Love," King-Kok Cheung (1990) contended that Chin and Chan buttressed patriarchy "by invoking gender stereotypes, by disparaging domestic efficiency as 'feminine,' and by slotting desirable traits such as originality, daring, physical courage, and creativity under the rubric of masculinity" (p. 237). Similarly, Wong (1993) argued that in their influential "Introduction" to *Aiiieeeee! An Anthology of Asian American Writers* (1974), Chan, Chin, Inada, and Wong operated on the premise that a true Asian American sensibility is "non-Christian, nonfeminine, and nonimmigrant" (p. 8).

Though limited and limiting, a masculinist cultural nationalist agenda appealed to Asian American activists because of its potential to oppose and disrupt the logic of racial domination. In the following excerpt, Elaine Kim (1993), a pioneer in the field of Asian American literature, explained the appeal of cultural nationalism:

> Certainly it was possible for me as a Korean American female to accept the fixed masculinist Asian American identity posited in Asian American cultural nationalism, even when it rendered invisible or at least muted women's oppression, anger, and ways of loving and interpreted Korean Americans as imperfect imitations of Chinese Americans; because I could see in everyday life that not all material and psychic violence to women of color comes from men, and because, as my friends used to say, "No Chinese [American] ever called me a 'Gook.' " (p. x)

Kim's statement suggests that for Asian American women, and for other women of color, gender is only a part of a larger pattern of unequal social relations. Despite the constraints of patriarchy, racism inscribes these women's lives and binds them to Asian American men in what Collins (1991) called a "love and trouble" tradition (p. 184).

Because the racial oppression of Asian Americans involves the "feminization" of Asian men (Said, 1979), Asian American women are caught between the need to expose the problems of male privilege and the desire to unite with men to contest the overarching racial ideology that confines them both. As Cheung (1990) suggested, Asian American women may be simultaneously sympathetic and angry toward the men in their ethnic community: sensitive to the men's marginality but resentful of their sexism (p. 239). Maxine Hong Kingston's writings seem to reflect these conflicting emotions. As discussed above, in the opening legend of *China Men*, the male protagonist Tang Ao is captured in the Land of Women (North America), where he is forced to become a woman—to have his feet bound, his ears pierced, his eyebrows plucked, his cheeks and lips painted. Cheung (1990) argued that this legend is double-edged, pointing not only to the racist debasement of Chinese Americans in their adopted country but also to the subjugation of Chinese women both in China and in the United States (p. 240). Although the effeminization suffered by Tang Ao is brutal, it is the same mutilation that many Chinese women were for centuries forced to bear. According to Goellnicht's (1992) reading of Kingston's work, this opening myth suggests that the author both deplores the emasculation of her forefathers by mainstream America and critiques the Confucian patriarchal practices of her ancestral homeland (p. 194). In *China Men*, Kingston also showed no acceptance of sexist practices by immigrant men. The father in this novel/autobiography is depicted as a broken man who attempts to reassert male authority by denigrating those who are even more powerless—the women and children in his family (Cheung, 1990, p. 241; Goellnicht, 1992, p. 200).

Along the same lines, Maxine Hong Kingston's *The Woman Warrior* (1977) reveals the narrator's contradictory attitudes toward her childhood "home," which is simultaneously a site of "woman hatred" and an area of resistance against the racism of the dominant culture. The community that nourishes her imagination and suffuses her with warmth is the same community that relegates women to an inferior position, limiting them to the role of serving men (Rabine, 1987, pp. 477-478). In the following passage, the narrator voices her mixed feelings toward the Chinese American community:

> I looked at their ink drawings of poor people snagging their neighbors' flotage with long flood hooks and pushing the girl babies on down the river. And I had to get out of hating range. . . . I refuse to shy my way anymore through our Chinatown, which tasks me with the old sayings and the stories. The swordswoman and I are not so dissimilar. May my people understand the resemblance so that I can return to them. (Kingston, 1977, p. 62)

Similarly, in a critique of Asian American sexual politics, Kayo Hatta's short video *Otemba* (1988) depicts a girl's-eye view of the final days of her mother's pregnancy as her father hopes and prays for the birth of a boy (see Tajima, 1991, p. 26).

Stripped of the privileges of masculinity, some Asian American men have attempted to reassert male authority by subordinating feminism to nationalist concerns. Lisa Lowe (1991) argued that this identity politics displaces gender differences into a false opposition of "nationalism" and "assimilation." From this limited perspective, Asian American feminists who expose Asian American sexism are cast as "assimilationist," as betraying Asian American "nationalism." Maxine Hong Kingston's *The Woman Warrior* (1977) and Amy Tan's *The Joy Luck Club* (1989) are the targets of such nationalist criticisms. Frank Chin, Ben Tong, and others have accused these and other women novelists of feminizing Asian American literature by exaggerating the community's patriarchal structure, thus undermining the power of Asian American men to combat the racist stereotypes of the dominant white culture. For example, when Kingston's *The Woman Warrior* received favorable reviews, Chin accused her of attempting to "cash in on the feminist fad" (Chan, 1994, p. 528). Another Asian American male had this to say about the movie *The Joy Luck Club:*

> The movie was powerful. But it could have been powerful *and inclusive,*
> if at least one of the Asian male characters was portrayed as something
> other than monstrously evil or simply wimpy. We are used to this
> message coming out of Hollywood, but it disturbed me deeply to hear
> the same message coming from Amy Tan and Wayne Wang—people of
> my own color. (Yoon, 1993)

Whereas Chin and others cast this tension in terms of nationalism and
assimilationism, Lisa Lowe (1991) argued that it is more a debate
between nationalist and feminist concerns in Asian American discourse.
This insistence on a fixed masculinist identity, according to Lowe
(1991), "can be itself a colonial figure used to displace the challenges of
heterogeneity, or subalternity, by casting them as assimilationist or
anti-ethnic" (pp. 33-34).

But cultural nationalism need not be patriarchal. Rejecting the ideology of oppositional dichotomous sex roles, Asian American cultural
workers have also engaged in cross-gender projects. In a recent review
of Asian American independent filmmaking, Renee Tajima (1991) reported that some of the best feminist films have been made by Asian
American men. For example, Arthur Dong's *Lotus* (1987) exposes women's
exploitation through the practice of footbinding (Tajima, 1991, p. 24).
Asian American men have also made use of personal documentary, in
both diary and autobiographical form—an approach known to be the
realm of women filmmakers. Finally, there is no particular gender
affiliation in subject matters: Just as Arthur Dong profiles his mother in
Sewing Woman, Lori Tsang portrays her father's life in *Chinaman's Choice*
(Tajima, 1991, p. 24).

Conclusion

Ideological representations of gender and sexuality are central in the
exercise and maintenance of racial, patriarchal, and class domination.
In the Asian American case, this ideological racism has taken seemingly
contrasting forms: Asian men have been cast as both hypersexual and
asexual, and Asian women have been rendered both superfeminine and
masculine. Although in apparent disjunction, both forms exist to define,
maintain, and justify white male supremacy. The racialization of Asian
American manhood and womanhood underscores the interconnections
of race, gender, and class. As categories of difference, race and gender
relations do not parallel but intersect and confirm each other, and it is
the complicity among these categories of difference that enables U.S.

elites to justify and maintain their cultural, social, and economic power. Responding to the ideological assaults on their gender identities, Asian American cultural workers have engaged in a wide range of oppositional projects to defend Asian American manhood and womanhood. In the process, some have embraced a masculinist cultural nationalism, a stance that marginalizes Asian American women and their needs. Though sensitive to the emasculation of Asian American men, Asian American feminists have pointed out that Asian American nationalism insists on a fixed masculinist identity, thus obscuring gender differences. Though divergent, both the nationalist and feminist positions advance the dichotomous stance of man or woman, gender or race or class, without recognizing the complex relationality of these categories of oppression. It is only when Asian Americans recognize the intersections of race, gender, and class that we can transform the existing hierarchical structure.

Notes

1. In 1996, the U.S. Congress deliberating on but did not pass two bills (S. 1394/269 and H.R. 2202) that would have sharply cut legal immigration by removing the family preferences from the existing immigration laws.

2. I thank Mary Romero for pointing this out to me.

3. Filipino Americans provide an exception in that Filipino American men tend to intermarry as frequently as Filipina American women. This is partly so because they are more Americanized and have a relatively more egalitarian gender-role orientation than other Asian American men (Agbayani-Siewert & Revilla, 1995, p. 156).

4. In recent years, Asian Americans' rising consciousness, coupled with their phenomenal growth in certain regions of the United States, has led to a significant increase in inter-Asian marriages (e.g., Chinese Americans to Korean Americans). In a comparative analysis of the 1980 and 1990 Decennial Census, Larry Hajimi Shinigawa and Gin Young Pang (forthcoming) found a dramatic decrease of interracial marriages and a significant rise of inter-Asian marriages. In California (where 39% of all Asian Pacific Americans reside), inter-Asian marriages increased from 21.1% in 1980 to 64% in 1990 of all intermarriages for Asian American husband, and from 10.8% to 45.% for Asian American wives during the same time period.

5. I thank Takeo Wong for calling my attention to this film.

CHAPTER 6

Beyond Dualisms

Constructing an Imagined Community

Societies tend to organize themselves around sets of mutually exclusive binaries: white or black, man or woman, professional or laborer, citizen or alien. In the United States, this binary construction of difference—of privileging and empowering the first term and reducing and disempowering the second—structures and maintains race, gender, and class privilege and power (Lowe, 1991, p. 31; Grosz, 1994, pp. 3-4). Thus, white/male/professional/citizen constitutes the norm against which black/female/laborer/alien is defined (Okihiro, 1995). Normed on this white, male, bourgeois hierarchy, working-class immigrant women of color are subordinated and suppressed (Mohanty, 1991, p. 6). There is also another kind of dualism, one that treats race, gender, and class as mutually exclusive categories. White feminist scholars engage in this either/or dichotomous thinking when they assert that gender oppression transcends divisions among women created by race, social class, and other forms of difference. Similarly, men of color rely on dualisms when they insist that the system of racial oppression takes precedence over that of gender oppression. By privileging *either* race *or* gender *or* class instead of recognizing their interconnections, this dichotomous stance marginalizes the experiences of those who are multiply disadvantaged (Crenshaw, 1990). As a multiply disadvantaged people, Asians in the United States complicate either/or definitions and categories and carve out for themselves a "third space" as "neither/nor" and as "both/ and" (Kim, 1993, p. viii). Because of their racial ambiguity, Asian Americans have been constructed historically to be *both* "like black" *and* "like white," as well as *neither* black *nor* white. Similarly, Asian women have been both hyperfemininized and masculinized, and Asian men have been both hypermasculinized and feminized. And in social class and cultural terms, Asian Americans have been cast both as the "unassimilable alien" and the "model minority" (Okihiro, 1995). Their ambiguous, middling positions maintain systems of privilege and power but also threaten and destabilize these constructs of hierarchies. This concluding chapter discusses how Asian Americans, as racialized "others" who occupy a "third" position, both disrupt and conform to the hegemonic dualisms of race, gender, and class.

Yellow as Neither Black nor White

The United States constructs a two-tiered racial order, with whites at one end and blacks at the other, and situates Asians (and other racial "others") somewhere along this black/white divide. As a "third" group, Asians have either been marginalized to the periphery of U.S. race relations or reinscribed within the black-white dyad as "near-blacks" (as in "cheap and exploitable labor"), or "near-whites" (as in "model minority"). But importantly, Asian Americans have also been constructed to be *neither* black *nor* white—and therein lies the source of their oppression. As members of both the "nonwhite other" and an intermediate group between black and white, Asian Americans have received some "special opportunities" but have also faced "unique disabilities" (Okihiro, 1994, p. xi).

Although both African and Asian Americans have been suppressed and subordinated as "nonwhite," white Americans have also differentiated between these two groups. In the post-Civil War South, Chinese laborers, as "aliens ineligible to citizenship," were used to discipline the newly enfranchised African workers and depress wages in the South. Asian laborers were deemed ideal replacements for African slaves not only because of their alien status but also because they were neither black nor white. As an intermediate group, Asians insulated whites from blacks and thus both mediated and advanced the prevailing social hierarchy (Loewen, 1971). By declaring Asian immigrants "aliens ineligible to citizenship," white Americans cast Asian immigrants as "almost blacks but not blacks." In contrast, the contemporary model-minority stereotype, which proclaims Asian Americans to be the minority whose success affirms the status quo, renders them as "almost whites but not whites." Although Asian Americans are lauded for their alleged successes, they continue to face white racism in the political, economic, and social arenas as well as white resentment and violence for being "too successful"—thus reminding them that they are indeed not whites (Okihiro, 1994, chap. 2). Moreover, these two images—the perpetual alien and the model minority—are linked. The "alienness" of Asian Americans, as constructed by the U.S. legal and cultural systems, has rendered them among the most exploitable and exploited workers in the United States, thus leading to white designation of Asians as "favored workers" (i.e., the model minority; Hossfeld, 1994, p. 70). In other words, it is their exploitability, rather than their cultural superiority, that explains employers' supposed preference to hire Asians.

As neither black nor white, Asians are also unmistakably "yellow" and embody for many other Americans the Yellow Peril—a military, economic, and social threat to the United States. This irrational fear, with its racist and sex-fantasy overtones, has circumscribed the fate of Asians in the United States, particularly during World War II, when Japanese Americans and then Chinese Americans were punished for their alleged affiliation with and loyalty to the menacing Orientals. The Yellow Peril image also brands Asians as unassimilable aliens—perpetual foreigners who disqualify themselves from full American membership by questionable political allegiance and outlandish Oriental cultures (Wong, 1993, p. 6). Distinguishing this culture-based oppression from the skin-color-based discrimination faced by African Americans, Sonia Shah (1994) asserted that "the formative discrimination in my life has resulted from culturally different (not necessarily racially different) people thinking they were culturally central: thinking that *my* house smelled funny, that *my* mother talked weird, that *my* habits were strange. They were normal; I wasn't" (pp. 151-152). In other words, the notion of the Yellow Peril constructs Asian culture to be the "other," not only different from but inferior to white standards. As Ruth Frankenberg (1993) argued, "Whiteness often stood as an unmarked marker of others' differentness" (p. 198). The idea of the unassimilable alien marks Asian Americans, once again, as neither black nor white, and, in so doing, it normalizes and rationalizes the existing racial order and keeps race privilege from being fully recognized, acknowledged, and therefore ended.

Asians as Neither Man nor Woman

Definitions of gender norms in the United States are based on the experiences of middle-class white men and white women. In the idealized American family, women are full-time homemakers and mothers, and men are the breadwinners. U.S. culture portrays these gender roles—the bread baker and the breadwinner—as complementary, ignoring the historical and political context of their constructions and gliding over questions of power and conflict (Romero, 1992, p. 17). This naturalized sexual division of labor engenders other sex-specific stereotypes: Men are independent, capable, powerful, whereas women are dependent, ineffectual, and weak. As such, men become the protectors and women the protected. These white-constructed gender norms form a backdrop of expectations for men and women of color—expectations that racism often precludes meeting (Crenshaw, 1989, 155). In general, men of color are depicted not as protectors, but rather as aggressors—threats to white women (Davis, 1981). Women of color are portrayed as oversexualized and thus undeserving of the social and sexual protection accorded to white middle-class women (Davis, 1981; Crenshaw, 1989). For Asian American men and women, exclusion from white-based cultural notions of the masculine and the feminine has taken seemingly contrasting forms: Asian men have been cast as both hypermasculine and feminine, and Asian women have been rendered both superfeminine and masculine.

Throughout the history of Asians in the United States, but particularly prior to the enactment of anti-Asian immigration laws, U.S. popular media consistently depicted Asian men as a sexual danger to virginal white women. The racist portrayals of Asian men as licentious and predatory were especially virulent during the nativist movement against Asians at the turn of the century (Frankenberg, 1993, pp. 75-76). The exclusion of Asian women from the United States and the subsequent establishment of womanless households eventually inverted the construction of Asian masculinity from "hypersexual" to "undersexed" or "effeminate." Cinematically, Asian men were depicted as neuter; they could not sexually engage white women, and, when juxtaposed with white men, could not engage Asian women. The desexualization of the Asian male naturalized the absence of conjugal families in the United States and constructed a reality in which discrimination against these men appeared defensible.

The material existence of Asian American men has also been historically at odds with the traditional construction of "man." During the pre-World War II period, racialized and gendered immigration policies and labor conditions emasculated Asian men, forcing them into womanless communities and into "feminized jobs" that had gone unfilled due to the absence of women. The existence of the Asian laundryman and waiter further bolstered the myth of the effeminate or androgynous Asian man. Feminization, in turn, confined Asian immigrant men to the sector of the state's labor force that performed "feminized" work. Cheung (1990) suggested that the mistreatment of Asian men during this period took the form of sexism, in that the injustices endured by these men were remarkably similar to those traditionally suffered by women (p. 224). Like women, Asian men were disenfranchised, denied the right to citizenship, prohibited from owning land or real estate, forced to attend segregated schools, and barred from speaking in court. During World War II, the internment of Japanese Americans stripped Issei men of their role as the family breadwinner, transferred some of their power and status to the U.S.-born children, and decreased male dominance over women. In the contemporary period, the patriarchal authority of Asian immigrant men, particularly those of the working class, has also been challenged due to the social and economic losses that they suffered in the transition to life in the United States. The current image of the model minority further casts Asian American men as passive and malleable— and thus as "feminine" (Okihiro, 1994, pp. 141-142).

White-constructed gender norms have also excluded Asian American women. While white women have been portrayed as chaste and dependable, Asian women in the past have been represented as promiscuous and untrustworthy. In a mirror image of the evil Oriental man, Asian women were cast as the castrating Dragon Lady—a deceitful, dangerous, and treacherous creature who poisons a man as easily as she seduces him. Indeed, at the turn of the century, the public perception of Chinese women as disease-ridden, opium-addicted prostitutes played a decisive role in the eventual passage of exclusion laws against them. According to Sucheng Chan (1991b), the stereotypical view that all Chinese women were prostitutes, first formed in the 1850s and continued for almost a century, colored public perceptions of, attitudes toward, and actions against all Chinese women, regardless of their social standing (p. 132). Moreover, unlike middle-class white women, Asian women have historically been denied access to a "normative family," the traditional locus for the construction of womanhood. For example, in the pre-World War II era, Asian women endured a split-household arrangement: They were lonely wives and forlorn mothers who presided over empty households while their husbands and grown children toiled in the distant United States. In a similar fashion, Issei women who were interned during World War II were driven from their homes and thus were stripped of their domestic responsibilities and their position as "queen of the house." Finally, most Asian women have had to work outside the home to supplement their husbands' incomes. The very fact that Asian American women must work conflicts with gender norms that women should not. As racialized feminized labor, Asian immigrant and Asian American women have constituted a low-paid and masculinized workforce, often performing heavy "men's work" in the farms, in textile and garment industries, and in hotels and restaurants. The international growth of female-intensive industries—or in Lisa Lowe's (1996) term, the "racialized feminization of labor"—further masculinizes Asian women by enhancing their employability over men and changing their role to that of a co-provider, if not primary provider, for the financial well-being of the family.

At the other extreme, Asian women have been fetishized in recent years as the embodiment of perfect womanhood and genuine exotic femininity. Marchetti (1993) argued that the Western construction of the passive Asian beauty as the feminine ideal upholds white masculine hegemony (pp. 134-135). Cast as the "superfemme," Asian women are idealized to be more truly "feminine" (i.e., devoted, dependent, domestic), and therefore more desirable, than their more modern, emancipated Western sisters. In pitting Asian women against white women, U.S. popular culture affirms white male identity against the threat of emerging feminism by warning white women to return to the "feminine sphere"—to their duties of wife and mother—if they wish to attract and keep a man. It is important to note that as the racialized "exotic treasure," Asian women do not replace but merely function as a temporary "stand-in" for white women and thus will be readily displaced if and when the "real" woman returns.

In sum, materially and culturally, Asian American men and women have been cast as *both* men *and* women and as *neither* men *nor* women. On the one hand, as part of the Yellow Peril that needs to be contained, Asian men and women have been represented as a *masculine* threat of military and sexual dominance and moral degeneracy. On the other hand, both sexes have been skewed toward the female side—a manifestation of the group's marginalization and its role as the passive "model minority" in contemporary U.S. cultural lore (Okihiro, 1994, pp. 141-142). The feminization and masculinization of Asian men and women serve the same function: Both exist to define, maintain, and justify white male privilege (Kim, 1990, p. 70).

Race or Gender or Class

The problems of race, gender, and class are closely intertwined in the lives of Asian American men and women. It is racial and class

oppression against "yellows" that restricts their material lives, (re)de-
fines their gender roles, and provides material for degrading and exaggerated sexual representations of Asian men and women in U.S. popular culture. Asian Americans have always, but particularly since the
1960s, resisted race, class, and gender exploitation through political,
economic, and cultural activism. As a result, the objectification of Asian
Americans as exotic aliens who are different from, and inferior to, white
Americans has never been absolute.

On the other hand, in demanding legitimacy, some Asian Americans
have adopted the either/or dichotomies of the dominant patriarchal
structure, "unwittingly upholding the criteria of those whom they
assail" (Cheung, 1990, p. 235). Lisa Lowe (1991) argued that "in accept-
ing the binary terms ('white' and 'nonwhite,' or 'majority' and 'minority') . . . , we forget that these binary schemas are not neutral descrip-
tions" (p. 31). For example, men who have been historically devalued
are likely to take their rage and frustration out on those closest to them
(Lipsitz, 1988, pp. 204-205; Crenshaw, 1990, pp. 185-189). Having been
forced into "feminine" subject positions, some Asian American men
seek to reassert their masculinity by physically and emotionally abusing those who are even more powerless: the women and children in
their families. In particular, men's inability to earn a family wage and
subsequent reliance on their wives' income undermines severely their
sense of well-being. Though it is useful to view male tyranny within the
context of racial inequality and class exploitation, it is equally important
to note that this aggression is informed by Eurocentric gender ideology,
particularly its emphasis on oppositional dichotomous sex roles. Because these Asian American men can see only race oppression, and not
gender domination, they are unable, or unwilling, to view themselves
as both oppressed and oppressor. This dichotomous stance has led to
the marginalization of Asian American women and their needs. Concerned with recuperating their identities as men and as Americans,
some Asian American political and cultural workers have subordinated
feminism to nationalist concerns. From this limited standpoint, Asian
American feminists who expose Asian American sexism are cast as
"anti-ethnic," criticized for undermining group solidarity, and charged
with exaggerating the community's patriarchal structure to please the
larger society. In an analysis of the display of machismo among Mexican
immigrant men, Pierrette Hondagneu-Sotelo (1994) characterized these
men's behaviors as "personally and collectively constructed perfor-
mances of masculine gender display . . . [which] should be distinguished

from structurally constituted positions of power" (pp. 193-194). In other words, these displays of male prowess are indicators of "marginalized and subordinated masculinities" (p. 194).

The racist debasement of Asian men makes it difficult for Asian American women to balance the need to expose the problems of male privilege with the desire to unite with men to contest the overarching racial ideology that confines them both. As Asian American women negotiate this difficult feat, they, like men, tend to subscribe to either/or dichotomous thinking. They do so when they adopt the fixed masculinist Asian American identity, even when it marginalizes their positions, or when they privilege women's concerns over men's or over concerns about other forms of inequality. Both of these positions advance the dichotomous stance of man or woman, gender or race or class, without recognizing the "complex *relationality* that shapes our social and political lives" (Mohanty, 1991, p. 13). Finally, Asian American women enforce Eurocentric gender ideology when they accept the objectification and feminization of Asian men and the parallel construction of white men as the most desirable sexual and marital partners.

Traditional white feminists likewise succumb to binary definitions and categories when they insist on the primacy of gender, thereby dismissing racism and other structures of oppression. The feminist mandate for gender solidarity accounts only for hierarchies between men and women and ignores power differentials among women, among men, and between white women and men of color. This exclusive focus on gender makes it difficult for white women to see the web of multiple oppressions that constrain the lives of most women of color, thus limiting the potential bonding among all women. Furthermore, it bars them from recognizing the oppression of men of color: the fact that there are men, and not only women, who have been "feminized" and the fact that white, middle class women hold cultural power and class power over certain groups of men (Cheung, 1990, pp. 245-246; Wiegman, 1991, p. 311).

In sum, Asian American men, Asian American women, and white women unwittingly comply with the ideologies of racialized patriarchy. Asian American men fulfill traditional definitions of manhood when they conflate might and masculinity and sweep aside the needs and well-being of Asian American women. Asian American women accept these racialized gender ideologies when they submit to white and Asian men or when they subordinate racial, class, or men's concerns to feminism. And white women advance a hierarchical agenda when they fail to see that the experiences of white women, women of color, and men of color are connected in systematic ways.

Beyond Dualisms:
Constructing an "Imagined Community"

As a multiply marginalized group, Asian Americans pose a fundamental problem to the binary oppositions that structure and maintain privilege and power in the United States (Okihiro, 1995). The conditions of their lives challenge the naturalisms of these dualisms and reveal how multiple structures of difference and disempowerment reinforce one another. In other words, they show how race, gender, and class, as categories of difference, do not parallel but instead intersect and confirm each other (Wiegman, 1991, p. 311). The task for feminist theory, then, is to develop paradigms that articulate the complicity among these categories of oppression, that strengthen the alliance between gender and ethnic studies, and that reach out not only to women, but perhaps also to men, of color (Cheung, 1990, p. 245).

A central task in feminist scholarship is to expose and dismantle the stereotypes that traditionally have provided ideological justifications for women's subordination. However, ideologies of manhood and womanhood have as much to do with class and race as they have to do with sex. Class and gender intersect when the culture of patriarchy, which assigns men to the public sphere and women to the private sphere, makes it possible for capitalists to exploit and profit from the labor of both men and women. Because patriarchy mandates that men be the breadwinners, it pressures them to work in the capitalist wage market, even in jobs that are low paying, physically punishing, and without opportunities for upward mobility. In this sense, the sexual division of labor within the family produces a steady supply of male labor for the benefits of capital. The culture of patriarchy is also responsible for the capitalist exploitation of women. The assumption that women are not the main income earners in their families, and therefore can afford to work for less, provides ideological justification for employers to hire women at lower wages and in poorer working conditions than exist for men (Hossfeld, 1994, p. 74). On the other hand, in however limited a way, wage employment does allow women to challenge the confines and dictates of traditional patriarchal social relations. It affords women some opportunities to leave the confines of the home, delay marriage and childbearing, develop new social networks, and exercise more personal independence (Lim, 1983, p. 83). As such, wage labor both oppresses and liberates women, exploiting them as workers but also strengthening their claims against patriarchal authority (Okihiro, 1994, p. 91). But this potential liberation is limited. As Linda Y. C. Lim (1983) pointed out, because capitalist employment and exploitation of female labor are based on patriarchal exploitation, "The elimination of these conditions may well bring about an elimination of the jobs themselves" (p. 88).

U.S. capital also profits from racism. In the pre-World War II era, white men were considered "free labor" and could take a variety of jobs in the industrialized economic sector, whereas Asian men were racialized as "coolie labor" and confined to nonunionized, degrading low-paying jobs in the agricultural and service sectors. Asian immigrants faced a special disability: They could not become citizens and thus were a completely disfranchised group. As noncitizens, Asian immigrants were subjected to especially onerous working conditions compared to other workers, including longer hours, lower wages, more physically demanding labor, and more dangerous tasks. The alien, and thus rights-deprived, status of Asian immigrants increased the ability of capital to control them; it also allowed employers to use the cheapness of Asian labor to undermine and discipline the white small producers and white workers (Bonacich, 1984, pp. 165-166). The post-1965 Asian immigrant group, though much more differentiated along social class lines, is still racialized and exploited. In all occupational sectors, Asian American men and women fare worse than their white counterparts. Unskilled and semiskilled Asian immigrant labor is relegated to the lower-paying job brackets of racially segregated industries. Due to their gender, race, and noncitizen status, Asian immigrant women fare the worst because they are seen as being the most desperate for work at any wage (Hossfeld, 1994, p. 75). The highly educated, on the other hand, encounter institutionalized economic and cultural racism that restricts their economic mobility. In sum, capitalist exploitation of Asians has been possible mainly because Asian labor had already been categorized by a racist society as being worth less than white workers' labor. This racial hierarchy then confirms the "manhood" of white men while rendering Asian men impotent.

Racist economic exploitation of Asian American men has had gender implications. Due to the men's inability to earn a family wage, Asian American women have had to engage in paid labor to make up the income discrepancies. In other words, the racialized exploitation of

Asian American men has historically been the context for the entry of Asian American women into the labor force. Access to wage work and relative economic independence, in turn, has given women solid ground for questioning their subordination. But progress has been slow and uneven. In some instances, more egalitarian divisions of labor and control of domestic resources have emerged. In others, men's loss of status in the public and domestic spheres has placed severe pressures on the traditional family, leading at times to resentment, verbal or physical abuse, and divorce.

Moreover, Asian women's ability to transform traditional patriarchy is often constrained by their social-structural location in the dominant society. The articulation between the processes of gender discrimination, racial discrimination of (presumed or actual) immigrant workers, and capitalist exploitation makes their position particularly vulnerable. Constrained by these overlapping categories of oppression, Asian American women may accept certain components of the traditional patriarchal system to have a strong and intact family—an important source of support to sustain them in the work world (Glenn, 1986; Kibria, 1990). Indeed, in this hostile environment, the act of maintaining families is itself a form of resistance. Finally, women's economic resources have remained too meager for them to maintain their economic independence from men. Therefore, some Asian American women may choose to preserve the traditional family system, though in a tempered form, because they value the promise of male economic protection. As Evelyn Nakano Glenn (1986) pointed out, for Asian Americans, the family has been "simultaneously a unity, bound by interdependence in the fight for survival, and a segmented institution in which men and women struggled over power, resources, and labor" (p. 218).

* * *

To recognize the interconnections of race, gender, and class is also to recognize that the conditions of our lives are connected to and shaped by the conditions of others' lives. Thus, men are privileged precisely because women are not, and whites are advantaged precisely because people of color are disadvantaged. In other words, both people of color and white people live racially structured lives, both women's and men's lives are shaped by their gender, and all of our lives are influenced by the dictates of the patriarchal economy of U.S. society (Wiegman, 1991, p. 311; Frankenberg, 1993, p. 1). But the intersections among these categories of oppression mean that there are also hierarchies among women and among men and that some women hold cultural and economic power over certain groups of men. On the other hand, the "intersecting, contradictory, and cross-category functioning of U.S. culture" (Wiegman, 1991, p. 331) also presents opportunities for transforming the existing hierarchical structure. If Asian men have been "feminized" in the United States, then they can best attest to and fight against patriarchal oppression that has long denied all women male privilege. If white women recognize that ideologies of womanhood have as much to do with race and class as they have to do with sex, then they can better work with, and not for, women (and men) of color. And if men and women of all social classes understand how capitalism distorts and diminishes all peoples' lives, then they will be more apt to struggle together for a more equitable economic system. Thus, to name the categories of oppression and to identify their interconnections is also to explore, forge, and fortify cross-gender, cross-racial, and cross-class alliances. It is to construct what Chandra Mohanty (1991) called an "imagined community" (p. 4): a community that is bounded not only by color, race, gender, or class but crucially by a shared struggle against *all* pervasive and systemic forms of domination.

Agbayani-Siewert, P., & Revilla, L. (1995). Filipino Americans. In P. G. Min (Ed.), *Asian Americans: Contemporary trends and issues* (pp. 134-168). Thousand Oaks, CA: Sage.

Akast, D. (1993, March 9). Cruller fates: Cambodians find slim profit in doughnuts. *Los Angeles Times*, p. D1.

American Sociological Association, Committee on the Status of Women in Sociology. (1985). *The treatment of gender in research*. Washington, DC: Author.

Amott, T., & Matthaei, J. (1991). *Race, gender, and work: A multicultural economic history of women in the United States*. Boston: South End.

Asis, M. M. B. (1991). *To the United States and into the labor force: Occupational expectations of Filipino and Korean immigrant women* (Papers of the East-West Institute, No. 118). Honolulu: East-West Center.

Baca Zinn, M., & Dill, B. T. (1994). Difference and domination. In M. Baca Zinn & B. T. Dill (Eds.), *Women of color in U.S. society* (pp. 3-12). Philadelphia: Temple University Press.

Baker, D. G. (1983). *Race, ethnicity, and power: A comparative study*. New York: Routledge.

Beneria, L., & Roldan, M. (1987). *The crossroads of class and gender*. Chicago: University of Chicago Press.

Bich, N. N. (Ed.). (1989). *War and exile: A Vietnamese anthology*. Springfield, VA: Vietnam PEN Abroad.

Bonacich, E. (1984). Asian labor in the development of Hawaii and California. In L. Cheng & E. Bonacich (Eds.), *Labor immigration under capitalism: Asian workers in the United States before World War II* (pp. 130-185). Berkeley: University of California Press.

Bonacich, E. (1994). Asians in the Los Angeles garment industry. In P. Ong, E. Bonacich, & L. Cheng (Eds.), *The new Asian immigration in Los Angeles and global restructuring* (pp. 137-163). Berkeley: University of California Press.

Bonacich, E., & Cheng, L. (1984). Introduction: A theoretical orientation to international labor migration. In L. Cheng & E. Bonacich (Eds.), *Labor immigration under capitalism: Asian workers in the United States before World War II* (pp. 1-56). Berkeley: University of California Press.

Bonacich, E., Hossain, M., & Park, J. (1987). Korean immigrant working women in the early 1980s. In E. Yu & E. H. Philipps (Eds.), *Korean women in transition: At home and abroad* (pp. 219-247). Los Angeles: California State University, Center for Korean-American and Korean Studies.

Broom, L., & Riemer, R. (1949). *Removal and return: The socio-economic effects of the war on Japanese Americans.* Berkeley: University of California Press.

Bulosan, C. (1973). *America is in the heart: A personal history.* Seattle: Washington University Press. (Original work published 1946)

Campomanes, O. (1992). Filipinos in the United States and their literature of exile. In S. G. Lim & A. Ling (Eds.), *Reading the literatures of Asian America* (pp. 49-78). Philadelphia: Temple University Press.

Castillo, G. (1979). *Beyond Manila: Philippine rural problems in perspective.* Ottawa: International Development Research Centre.

Cha, T. H. K. (1982). *Dictee.* New York: Tanam.

Chai, A. Y. (1987). Freed from the elders but locked into labor: Korean immigrant women in Hawaii. *Women's Studies, 13,* 223-234.

Chan, J. P., Chin, F., Inada, L. F., & Wong, S. (1974). *Aiiieeeee! An anthology of Asian American writers.* Washington, DC: Howard University Press.

Chan, S. (1989). New studies in ethnicity, gender, and political inequality. In S. Chan (Ed.), *Social and gender boundaries in the United States* (pp. 1-35). Lewiston, NY: Edwin Mellen.

Chan, S. (1991a). *Asian Americans: An interpretive history.* Boston: Twayne.

Chan, S. (1991b). The exclusion of Chinese women. In S. Chan (Ed.), *Entry denied: Exclusion and the Chinese community in America, 1882-1943* (pp. 94-146). Philadelphia: Temple University Press.

Chan, S. (1994). The Asian American movement, 1960s-1980s. In S. Chan, D. H. Daniels, M. T. Garcia, & T. P. Wilson (Eds.), *Peoples of color in the American West* (pp. 525-533). Lexington, MA: D. C. Heath.

Chen, H.-S. (1992). *Chinatown no more: Taiwan immigrants in contemporary New York.* Ithaca, NY: Cornell University Press.

Chen, M. Y. (1976). Teaching a course on Asian American women. In E. Gee (Ed.), *Counterpoint: Perspectives on Asian America* (pp. 234-239). Los Angeles: University of California at Los Angeles, Asian American Studies Center.

Cheng, L. (1984). Free, indentured, enslaved: Chinese prostitutes in nineteenth-century America. In L. Cheng & E. Bonacich (Eds.), *Labor immigration under capitalism: Asian workers in the United States before World War II* (pp. 402-430). Berkeley: University of California Press.

Cheung, K.-K. (1990). The woman warrior versus the Chinaman pacific: Must a Chinese American critic choose between feminism and heroism? In M. Hirsch & E. F. Keller (Eds.), *Conflicts in feminism* (pp. 234-251). New York: Routledge.

Chin, F. (1972). Confessions of the Chinatown cowboy. *Bulletin of Concerned Asian Scholars, 4*(3), 66.

Chin, F., & Chan, J. P. (1972). Racist love. In R. Kostelanetz (Ed.), *Seeing through shuck* (pp. 65-79). New York: Ballantine.

Chinn, T. (1989). *Bridging the Pacific: San Francisco Chinatown and its people.* San Francisco: Chinese Historical Society of America.

Chiswick, B. (1979). The economic progress of immigrants: Some apparently universal patterns. In W. Fellner (Ed.), *Contemporary economic problems* (pp. 357-399). Washington, DC: American Enterprise Institute.

Choe, Laura. 1996, February 10. "Versions": Asian Americans in Hip Hop. Paper presented at the California Studies Conference, Long Beach, CA.

Chow, E. N.-L. (1987). The development of feminist consciousness among Asian American women. *Gender and Society, 1,* 284-299.

Chow, E. N.-L. (1994). Asian American women at work. In M. Baca Zinn & B. T. Dill (Eds.), *Women of color in U.S. society* (pp. 203-227). Philadelphia: Temple University Press.

Chu, L. (1961). *Eat a bowl of tea.* Seattle: University of Washington Press.

Collins, P. H. (1990). *Black feminist thought: Knowledge, consciousness, and the politics of empowerment.* New York: Routledge.

Coolidge, M. R. (1968). *Chinese immigration.* New York: Henry Holt. (Original work published 1909)

Crenshaw, K. (1989). Demarginalizing the intersection of race and sex: A black feminist critique of antidiscrimination doctrine, feminist theory and antiracist politics. In *University of Chicago Legal Forum: Feminism in the law: Theory, practice, and criticism* (pp. 139-167). Chicago: University of Chicago Press.

Curtis, R. (1986). Household and family in theory on equality. *American Sociological Review, 51*(2), 168-183.

Daniels, R. (1988). *Asian America: Chinese and Japanese in the United States since 1850.* Seattle: University of Washington Press.

Dasgupta, S. D. (1985). Marching to a different drummer? Sex role orientation of Indian women in the U.S. *Committee on South Asian Women Bulletin,* pp. 15-17.

Davis, A. (1981). *Women, race, and class.* New York: Random House.

Dhaliwal, A. K. (1995). Gender at work: The renegotiation of middle-class womanhood in a South Asian-owned business. In W. L. Ng, S.-Y. Chin, J. S. Moy, & G. Y. Okihiro (Eds.), *Reviewing Asian America: Locating diversity* (pp. 75-85). Pullman: Washington State University Press.

Dill, B. T. (1994). Fictive kin, paper sons, and compadrazgo: Women of color and the struggle for family survival. In M. Baca Zinn & B. T. Dill (Eds.), *Women of color in U.S. society* (pp. 149-169). Philadelphia: Temple University Press.

Doane, M. A. (1991). *Femme fatales: Feminism, film theory, psychoanalysis*. New York: Routledge.

Donato, K. M. (1992). Understanding U.S. immigration: Why some countries send women and others send men. In D. Gabaccia (Ed.), *Seeking common ground: Multidisciplinary studies of immigrant women in the United States* (pp. 159-184). Westport, CT: Greenwood.

Donato, K. M., & Tyree, A. (1986). Family reunification, health professionals, and the sex composition of immigrants to the United States. *Social Science Review, 70*, 226-230.

Dong, A. (Director). (1982). *Sewing woman* [Film]. San Francisco: DeepFocus Productions.

Donnelly, N. D. (1994). *Changing lives of refugee Hmong women*. Seattle: Washington University Press.

Duleep, H., & Sanders, S. (1993). Discrimination at the top: American-born Asian and white men. *Industrial Relations, 31*, 416-432.

Engelhardt, T. (1976). Ambush at Kamikaze Pass. In E. Gee (Ed.), *Counterpoint: Perspectives on Asian America* (pp. 270-279). Los Angeles: University of California at Los Angeles, Asian American Studies Center.

Espiritu, Y. L. (1992). *Asian American panethnicity: Bridging institutions and identities*. Philadelphia: Temple University Press.

Espiritu, Y. L. (1995). *Filipino American lives*. Philadelphia: Temple University Press.

Fawcett, J. T., & Gardner, R. W. (1994). Asian immigrant entrepreneurs and non-entrepreneurs: A comparative study of recent Korean and Filipino immigrants. *Population and Environment, 15*, 211-238.

Feria, R. T. (1946-1947). War and the status of Filipino immigrants. *Sociology and Social Research, 31*, 48-53.

Frankenberg, R. (1993). *White women, race matters: The social construction of whiteness*. Minneapolis: University of Minnesota Press.

Fung, R. (1994). Seeing yellow: Asian identities in film and video. In K. Aguilar-San Juan (Ed.), *The state of Asian America* (pp. 161-171). Boston: South End.

Gabaccia, D. (1992). Introduction. In D. Gabaccia (Ed.), *Seeking common ground: Multidisciplinary studies of immigrant women in the United States* (pp. xi-xxvi). Westport, CT: Greenwood.

Gaines, J. (1990). White privilege and looking relations: Race and gender in feminist film theory. In P. Erens (Ed.), *Issues in feminist film criticism* (pp. 197-214). Bloomington: Indiana University Press.

Gardner, R., Robey, B., & Smith, P. C. (Eds.). (1985). Asian Americans: Growth, change, and diversity [special issue]. *Population Bulletin, 40*(4).

Gensui, N. (1976). Footprints: Poetry of the American relocation experience (translated by Constance Hayashi and Keiho Yamanaka). *Amerasia Journal, 3,* 115-117.

Gentry, C. (1964). *Madames of San Francisco.* New York: Doubleday.

Glenn, E. N. (1983, February). Split household, small producer and dual wage earner: An analysis of Chinese-American family strategies. *Journal of Marriage and the Family, 45,* 35-46.

Glenn, E. N. (1986). *Issei, Nisei, war bride: Three generations of Japanese American women at domestic service.* Philadelphia: Temple University Press.

Glenn, E. N. (1992). From servitude to service work: Historical continuities in the racial division of paid reproductive labor. *Signs: Journal of Women in Culture and Society, 18,* 1-43.

Goellnicht, D. C. (1992). Tang Ao in America: Male subject positions in *China Men.* In S. G. Lim & A. Ling (Eds.), *Reading the literatures of Asian America* (pp. 191-212). Philadelphia: Temple University Press.

Gold, S. (1988). Refugees and small business: The case of Soviet Jews and Vietnamese. *Ethnic and Racial Studies, 11,* 411-438.

Gold, S. (1994). Chinese Vietnamese entrepreneurs in California. In P. Ong, E. Bonacich, & L. Cheng (Eds.), *The new Asian immigration in Los Angeles and global restructuring* (pp. 196-226). Philadelphia: Temple University Press.

Gold, S., & Kibria, N. (1993). Vietnamese refugees and blocked mobility. *Asian and Pacific Migration Review, 2,* 27-56.

Grosz, E. (1994). *Volatile bodies: Toward a corporeal feminism.* Bloomington: Indiana University Press.

Guttentag, M., & Secord, P. F. (1983). *Too many women? The sex ratio question.* Newbury Park, CA: Sage.

Hagedorn, J. (1993). Introduction: "Role of dead man require very little acting." In J. Hagedorn (Ed.), *Charlie Chan is dead: An anthology of contemporary Asian American fiction* (pp. xxi-xxx). New York: Penguin.

Hall, S. (1995). The whites of their eyes: Racist ideologies and the media. In G. Dines & J. M. Humez (Eds.), *Gender, race, and class in media* (pp. 18-22). Thousand Oaks, CA: Sage.

Hamamoto, D. Y. (1992). Kindred spirits: The contemporary Asian American family on television. *Amerasia Journal, 18*(2), 35-53.

Hamamoto, D. Y. (1994). *Monitored peril: Asian Americans and the politics of representation.* Minneapolis: University of Minnesota Press.

Harding, S. (1991). *Whose science? Whose knowledge?* Ithaca, NY: Cornell University Press.

Healey, J. F. (1995). *Race, ethnicity, gender, and class: The sociology of group conflict and change.* Thousand Oaks, CA: Pine Forge.

Hess, D. (1990). *Korean immigrant entrepreneurs in the Los Angeles garment industry.* Master's thesis, University of California, Los Angeles.

Hirata, L. C. (1976). The Chinese in American sociology. In E. Gee (Ed.), *Counterpoint: Perspectives on Asian America* (pp. 20-26). Los Angeles: University of California at Los Angeles, Asian American Studies Center.

Hirata, L. C. (1979). Chinese immigrant women in nineteenth-century California. In C. Berkin & M. Norton (Eds.), *Women of America* (pp. 223-244). Boston: Houghton Mifflin.

Hom, M. K. (1983). Some Cantonese folksongs on the American experience. *Western Folklore, 42,* 126-139.

Hondagneu-Sotelo, P. (1994). *Gendered transition: Mexican experiences in immigration.* Berkeley: University of California Press.

Hood, J. G. (1983). *Becoming a two job family.* New York: Praeger.

hooks, b. (1984). *Feminist theory: From margin to center.* Boston: South End.

Hoppenstand, G. (1983). Yellow devil doctors and opium dens: A survey of the yellow peril stereotypes in mass media entertainment. In C. D. Geist & J. Nachbar (Eds.), *The popular culture reader* (3rd ed., pp. 171-185). Bowling Green, OH: Bowling Green University Press.

Hossfeld, K. J. (1994). Hiring immigrant women: Silicon Valley's "simple formula." In M. Baca Zinn & B. T. Dill (Eds.), *Women of color in U.S. society* (pp. 65-93). Philadelphia: Temple University Press.

Houston, J. W., & Houston, J. D. (1973). *Farewell to Manzanar.* San Francisco: Houghton Mifflin.

Hsiao, R. Y. (1992). "Facing the incurable: Patriarchy in *Eat a Bowl of Tea.*" In S. G. Lim & A. Ling (Eds.), *Reading the literatures of Asian America* (pp. 151-162). Philadelphia: Temple University Press.

Hu-DeHart, E. (1993, September). The history, development, and future of ethnic studies. *Phi Delta Kappan, 74,* 50-54.

Hune, S. (1995). Rethinking race: Paradigms and policy formation. *Amerasia Journal, 21,* 29-40.

Hune, S. (1996). Doing gender in Asian American Studies: The space of difference that Asian American women make. Paper presented at the 13th national conference of the Association for Asian American Studies, Washington, DC.

Hurtado, A. (1989). Relating to privilege: Seduction and rejection in the subordination of white women and women of color. *Signs: Journal of Women in Culture and Society, 14,* 833-855.

Ichihashi, Y. (1932). *Japanese in the United States.* Stanford, CA: Stanford University Press.

Ichioka, Y. (1977). Japanese associations and the Japanese government: A special relationship, 1909-1926. *Pacific Historical Review, 46,* 409-437.

Ichioka, Y. (1980). *Amerika-Nadeshiko:* Japanese immigrant women in the United States, 1900-1924. *Pacific Historical Review, 44,* 339-357.

Ichioka, Y. (1988). *The Issei: The world of the first generation Japanese immigrants, 1885-1924.* New York: Free Press.

Irby, C., & Pon, E. M. (1988). Confronting new mountains: Mental health problems among male Hmong and Mien refugees. *Amerasia Journal, 14,* 109-118.

Ito, K. (1973). *Issei: A history of Japanese immigrants in North America.* Seattle: University of Washington Press.

Kang, Y. (1937). *East goes west.* New York: Scribner's.

Kanjanapan, W. (1995). The immigration of Asian professionals to the United States: 1988-1990. *International Migration Review, 29,* 7-32.

Katzman, D. (1978). Domestic service: Women's work. In A. Stromberg & S. Harkess (Eds.), *Women working: Theories and facts in perspective* (pp. 377-391). Palo Alto, CA: Mayfield.

Kibria, N. (1990). Power, patriarchy, and gender conflict in the Vietnamese immigrant community. *Gender & Society, 4,* 9-24.

Kibria, N. (1993). *Family tightrope: The changing lives of Vietnamese Americans.* Princeton, NJ: Princeton University Press.

Kikumura, A. (1981). *Through harsh winters: The life of a Japanese immigrant woman.* Novato, CA: Chandler & Sharp.

Kim, B.-L. (1972). Casework with Japanese and Korean wives of Americans. *Social Casework, 53,* 273-279.

Kim, B.-L. (1977). Asian wives of U.S. servicemen: Women in shadows. *Amerasia Journal, 4,* 91-115.

Kim, E. (1982). *Asian American literature: An introduction to the writings and their social context.* Philadelphia: Temple University Press.

Kim, E. (1984). Asian American writers: A bibliographical review. *American Studies International, 22,* 2.

Kim, E. (1990). "Such opposite creatures": Men and women in Asian American literature. *Michigan Quarterly Review, 29,* 68-93.

Kim, E. (1993). Preface. In J. Hagedorn (Ed.), *Charlie Chan is dead: An anthology of contemporary Asian American fiction* (pp. vii-xiv). New York: Penguin.

Kim, K. C., & Hurh, W. M. (1985). Ethnic resource utilization of Korean immigrant entrepreneurs in the Chicago minority area. *International Migration Review, 19,* 82-111.

Kim, K. C., & Hurh, W. M. (1988). The burden of double roles: Korean wives in the U.S.A. *Ethnic and Racial Studies, 11,* 151-167.

Kingston, M. H. (1977). *The woman warrior.* New York: Vintage.

Kingston, M. H. (1980). *China men.* New York: Knopf.

Kitagawa, D. (1967). *Issei and Nisei: The internment years.* New York: Seabury.

Kitano, H. H. L. (1991a). The effects of the evacuation on the Japanese Americans. In R. Daniels, S. C. Taylor, & H. H. L. Kitano (Eds.), *Japanese Americans: From relocation to redress* (pp. 151-162). Seattle: University of Washington Press.

Kitano, H. H. L. (1991b). *Race relations.* Englewood Cliffs, NJ: Prentice Hall.

Kitano, H. H. L., & Daniels, R. (1988). *Asian Americans: Emerging minorities.* Englewood Cliffs, NJ: Prentice Hall.

Kwong, P. (1979). *Chinatown, N.Y.: Labor and politics, 1930-1950.* New York: Monthly Review.

La Brack, B. (1982). Immigration law and the revitalization process: The case of the California Sikhs. *Population Review, 25,* 59-66.

Lai, H. M. (1987). Historical development of the Chinese Consolidated Benevolent Association/*Huiguan* system. In (Ed.), *Chinese America: History and perspectives, 1987* (pp. 13-52). San Francisco: Chinese Historical Society of America.

Lai, T. (1992). Asian American women: Not for sale. In M. L. Andersen & P. H. Collins (Eds.), *Race, class, and gender: An anthology* (pp. 163-190). Belmont, CA: Wadsworth.

Lasker, B. (1969). *Filipino immigration to the United States and to Hawaii.* New York: Arno.

Lee, M. P. (1990). *Quiet odyssey: A pioneer Korean woman in America* (S. Chan, Ed.). Seattle: University of Washington Press.

Lee, R. H. (1956). The recent immigrant Chinese families of the San Francisco-Oakland area. *Marriage and Family Living, 18,* 14-24.

Leonard, K. (1982). Marriage and family life among early Asian Indian immigrants. *Population Review, 25,* 67-75.

Leong, R. (1995). Lived theory (notes on the run). *Amerasia Journal, 21,* v-x.

Light, I. (1972). *Ethnic enterprise in America: Business and welfare among Chinese, Japanese, and blacks.* Berkeley: University of California Press.

Light, I., & Bonacich, E. (1986). *Immigrant entrepreneurs: Koreans in Los Angeles, 1965-1982.* Berkeley: University of California Press.

Lim, L. Y. C. (1983). Capitalism, imperialism, and patriarchy: The dilemma of Third-World women workers in multinational factories. In J. Nash & M. P. Fernandez-Kelly (Eds.), *Women, men, and the international division of labor* (pp. 70-91). Albany: State University of New York Press.

Ling, A. (1990). *Between worlds: Women writers of Chinese ancestry.* New York: Pergamon.

Ling, S. H. (1989). The mountain movers: Asian American women's movement in Los Angeles. *Amerasia Journal, 15,* 51-67.

Lipsitz, G. (1988). *A life in the struggle: Ivory Perry and the culture of opposition.* Philadelphia: Temple University Press.

Liu, J. M., Ong, P. M., & Rosenstein, C. Dual chain migration: Post-1965 Filipino immigration to the United States. *International Migration Review, 25,* 487-517.

Loewen, J. (1971). *The Mississippi Chinese: Between black and white.* Cambridge, MA: Harvard University Press.

Loo, C., & Ong, P. (1982). Slaying demons with a sewing needle: Feminist issues for Chinatown's women. *Berkeley Journal of Sociology, 27,* 77-88.

Louie, M. C. (1992). Immigrant Asian women in Bay Area garment shops: "After sewing, laundry, cleaning and cooking, I have no breath left to sing." *Amerasia Journal, 18,* 1-26.

Lowe, L. (1991). Heterogeneity, hybridity, multiplicity: Marking Asian American difference. *Diaspora, 1,* 24-44.

Lowe, L. (1994). Canon, institutionalization, identity: Contradictions for Asian American studies. In D. Palumbo-Liu (Ed.), *The ethnic canon: Histories, institutions, and interventions* (pp. 48-68). Minneapolis: University of Minnesota Press.

Lowe, L. (1996). *Immigrant acts: On Asian American cultural politics.* Durham, NC: Duke University Press.

Luu, V. (1989). The hardships of escape for Vietnamese women. In Asian Women United of California (Ed.), *Making waves: An anthology of writings by and about Asian American women* (pp. 60-72). Boston: Beacon.

Lyman, S. (1968). Marriage and the family among Chinese immigrants to America, 1850-1960. *Phylon, 19,* 321-330.

Lyman, S. (1974). Conflict and the web of group affiliation in San Francisco's Chinatown, 1850-1910. *Pacific Historical Review, 43,* 473-499.

Mar, D., & Kim, M. (1994). Historical trends. In P. Ong (Ed.), *The state of Asian Pacific America: Economic diversity, issues, and policies* (pp. 13-30). Los Angeles: LEAP Asian Pacific American Public Policy Institute and University of California at Los Angeles, Asian American Studies Center.

Marchetti, G. (1993). *Romance and the "Yellow Peril": Race, sex, and discursive strategies in Hollywood fiction.* Berkeley: University of California Press.

Matsui, R. (1987, September 17). Speech in the House of Representatives on the 442 bill for redress and reparations. *Cong. Rec.* 7584. Washington, DC: Government Printing Office.

Matsumoto, V. (1989). Nisei women and resettlement during World War II. In Asian Women United of California (Ed.), *Making waves: An anthology of writings by and about Asian American women* (pp. 115-126). Boston: Beacon.

May, L. (1987, February 2). Asians looking to broaden horizons: Immigrants prosper but hope to venture outside the "business ghetto." *Los Angeles Times*.

Mazumdar, S. (1989). General introduction: A woman-centered perspective on Asian American history. In Asian Women United of California (Ed.), *Making waves: An anthology by and about Asian American women* (pp. 1-22). Boston: Beacon.

Min, P. G. (1992). Korean immigrant wives' overwork. *Korea Journal of Population and Development, 21*, 23-36.

Min, P. G. (1995). Korean Americans. In P. G. Min (Ed.), *Asian Americans: Contemporary trends and issues* (pp. 199-231). Thousand Oaks, CA: Sage.

Modell, J. (Ed.). (1973). *The Kikuchi diary: Chronicle from an American concentration camp*. Urbana: University of Illinois Press.

Mohanty, C. T. (1991). Cartographies of struggle: Third World women and the politics of feminism. In C. T. Mohanty, A. Russo, & L. Torres (Eds.), *Third World women and the politics of feminism* (pp. 1-47). Bloomington: University of Indiana Press.

Montero, D. (1980). *Vietnamese Americans: Patterns of resettlement and socioeconomic adaptation in the United States*. Boulder, CO: Westview.

Moore, J., & Pachon, H. (1989). *Hispanics in the United States*. Prentice Hall.

Moraga, C. (1981). Preface. In C. Moraga & G. Anzaldua (Eds.), *This bridge called my back: Writings by radical women of color* (pp. xiii-xix). Watertown, MA: Persephone.

Moriyama, A. T. (1985). *Imingaisha: Japanese emigration companies and Hawaii*. Honolulu: University of Hawaii Press.

Morokvasic, M. (1984). Birds of passage are also women. *International Migration Review, 18*, 886-907.

Mullings, L. (1994). Images, ideology, and women of color. In M. Baca Zinn & B. T. Dill (Eds.), *Women of color in U.S. society* (pp. 265-289). Philadelphia: Temple University Press.

Myrdal, G. (1944). *An American dilemma*. New York: Harper & Brothers.

Nakano, M. T. (1990). *Japanese American women: Three generations, 1890-1990*. Berkeley, CA: Mina.

Nee, V., & Nee, B. B. (1973). *Longtime Californ': A documentary study of an American Chinatown*. New York: Pantheon.

Nee, V., & Wong, H. (1985). Asian American achievement: The strength of the family bond. *Sociological Perspectives, 28*, 281-306.

Nguyen, V. (1990, December 7). Growing up in white America. *Asian Week*, p. 23.

Nishi, S. M. (1995). Japanese Americans. In P. G. Min (Ed.), *Asian Americans: Contemporary trends and issues* (pp. 95-133). Thousand Oaks, CA: Sage.

Nomura, G. (1989). Issei working women in Hawaii. In Asian Women United of California (Ed.), *Making waves: An anthology of writings by and about Asian American women* (pp. 135-148). Boston: Beacon.

Okada, J. (1957). *No-no boy*. Rutland, VT: Charles E. Tuttle.

Okazaki, S. (1995). *American Sons*. Promotional brochure for the film of that name.

Okihiro, G. Y. (1991). *Cane fires: The anti-Japanese movement in Hawaii, 1865-1945*. Philadelphia: Temple University Press.

Okihiro, G. Y. (1994). *Margins and mainstreams: Asians in American history and culture*. Seattle: University of Washington Press.

Okihiro, G. Y. (1995, November). *Reading Asian bodies, reading anxieties*. Paper presented at the University of California, San Diego Ethnic Studies Colloquium, La Jolla.

Omatsu, G. (1991). The themes of our epoch. *Amerasia Journal, 17*, 77-82.

Ong, P. (1984). Chinatown unemployment and the ethnic labor market. *Amerasia Journal, 11*, 35-54.

Ong, P. (1993). *Beyond Asian American poverty: Community economic development policies and strategies*. Los Angeles: LEAP.

Ong, P., & Azores, T. (1994a). Health professionals on the front-line. In P. Ong (Ed.), *The state of Asian Pacific America: Economic diversity, issues, and policies* (pp. 139-163). Los Angeles: LEAP Asian Pacific American Public Policy Institute and University of California at Los Angeles, Asian American Studies Center.

Ong, P., & Azores, T. (1994b). The migration and incorporation of Filipino nurses. In P. Ong, E. Bonacich, & L. Cheng (Eds.), *The new Asian immigration in Los Angeles and global restructuring* (pp. 164-195). Philadelphia: Temple University Press.

Ong, P., & Blumenberg, E. (1994). Scientists and engineers. In P. Ong (Ed.), *The state of Asian Pacific America: Economic diversity, issues, and policies* (pp. 165-189). Los Angeles: LEAP Asian Pacific American Public Policy Institute and University of California at Los Angeles, Asian American Studies Center.

Ong, P., Bonacich, E., & Cheng, L. (1994). The political economy of capitalist restructuring and the new Asian immigration. In P. Ong, E. Bonacich, & L. Cheng (Eds.), *The new Asian immigration in Los Angeles and global restructuring* (pp. 3-35). Philadelphia: Temple University Press.

Ong, P., & Hee, S. (1994). Economic diversity. In P. Ong (Ed.), *The state of Asian Pacific America: Economic diversity, issues, and policies* (pp. 31-56). Los Angeles: LEAP Asian Pacific American Public Policy Institute and University of California at Los Angeles, Asian American Studies Center.

Ong, P., & Umemoto, K. (1994). Life and work in the inner-city. In P. Ong (Ed.), *The state of Asian Pacific America: Economic diversity, issues, and policies* (pp. 87-112). Los Angeles: LEAP Asian Pacific American Public Policy Institute and University of California at Los Angeles, Asian American Studies Center.

Osumi, M. D. (1982). Asians and California's anti-miscegenation laws. In N. Tsuchida (Ed.), *Asian/Pacific American experiences: Women's perspectives* (pp. 1-37). Minneapolis: University of Minnesota, Asian/Pacific American Learning Resource Center and General College.

Park, K. (1989). Impact of new productive activities on the organization of domestic life: A case study of the Korean American community. In G. Nomura, R. Endo, S. Sumida, & R. Leong (Eds.), *Frontiers of Asian American studies* (pp. 140-150). Pullman: Washington State University Press.

Pascoe, P. (1990). *Relations of rescue: The search for female authority in the American West, 1874-1939.* New York: Oxford University Press, 1990.

Pedraza, S. (1991). Women and migration: The social consequences of gender. *Annual Review of Sociology, 17,* 303-325.

Peffer, G. A. (1986, Fall). Forbidden families: Emigration experiences of Chinese women under the Page Law, 1875-1882. *Journal of American Ethnic History, 6,* 28-46.

Peffer, G. A. (1992). From under the sojourner's shadow: A historiographical study of Chinese female immigration to America. *Journal of American Ethnic History, 2,* 41-67.

Personal Narratives Group. (1989). Origins: Personal Narratives Group. In Personal Narrative Group (Ed.), *Interpreting women's lives: Feminist theory and personal narratives* (pp. 3-15). Bloomington: Indiana University Press.

Pesquera, B. M. (1993). "In the beginning he wouldn't even lift a spoon": The division of household labor. In A. de la Torre & B. M. Pesquera (Eds.), *Building with our hands: New directions in Chicana studies* (pp. 181-195). Berkeley: University of California Press.

Pessar, P. R. (1984). The linkage between the household and workplace in the experience of Dominican immigrant women in the United States. *International Migration Review, 18,* 1188-1211.

Pido, A. J. A. (1986). *The Pilipinos in America: Macro/microdimensions of immigration and integration.* Staten Island, NY: Center for Migration Studies.

Portes, A., & Rumbaut, R. G. (1990). *Immigrant America: A portrait.* Berkeley: University of California Press.

Quinsaat, J. (1976). Asians in the media: The shadows in the spotlight. In E. Gee (Ed.), *Counterpoint: Perspectives on Asian America* (pp. 264-269). Los Angeles: University of California at Los Angeles, Asian American Studies Center.

Rabine, L. W. (1987). No lost paradise: Social gender and symbolic gender in the writings of Maxine Hong Kingston. *Signs: Journal of Women in Culture and Society, 12,* 471-511.

Romero, M. (1992). *Maid in the U.S.A.* New York: Routledge.

Rumbaut, R. (1995). Vietnamese, Laotian, and Cambodian Americans. In P. G. Min (Ed.), *Asian Americans: Contemporary trends and issues* (pp. 232-270). Thousand Oaks, CA: Sage.

Sacks, K. B., & Scheper-Hughes, N. (1987). Introduction. *Women's Studies, 13,* 175-182.

Said, E. (1979). *Orientalism.* New York: Random House.

Scharlin, C., & Villaneuva, L. V. (1992). *Philip Vera Cruz: A personal history of Filipino immigrants and the farmworkers movement.* Los Angeles: University of California at Los Angeles, Labor Center, Institute of Labor Relations and Asian American Studies Center.

Schnepp, G., & Yui, A. M. (1955). Cultural and marital adjustment of Japanese war brides. *American Journal of Sociology, 61,* 48-50.

Shah, S. (1994). Presenting the Blue Goddess: Toward a national, Pan-Asian feminist agenda. In K. Aguilar-San Juan (Ed.), *The state of Asian America: Activism and resistance in the 1990s* (pp. 147-158). Boston: South End.

Sharma, M. (1984). Labor migration and class formation among the Filipinos in Hawaii, 1906-1946. In L. Cheng & E. Bonacich (Eds.), *Labor immigration under capitalism: Asian workers in the United States before World War II* (pp. 579-611). Berkeley: University of California Press.

Shin, E. H., & Chang, K.-S. (1988). Peripheralization of immigrant professionals: Korean physicians in the United States. *International Migration Review, 22,* 609-626.

Siu, P. (1987). *The Chinese laundryman: A study in social isolation.* New York: New York University Press.

Sledge, L. C. (1980). Maxine Kingston's *China Men:* The family historian as epic poet. *MELUS, 7,* 3-22.

Srole, C. (1987). Converging paths: Korean and U.S. women 1900 to 1980s. In E.-Y. Yu & E. H. Phillips (Eds.), *Korean women in transition: At home and abroad* (pp. 1-13). Los Angeles: California State University at Los Angeles, Center for Korean-American and Korean Studies.

Stacey, J., & Thorne, B. (1985). The missing feminist revolution in sociology. *Social Problems, 32,* 301-316.

Strathorn, M. (1987). An awkward relationship: The case of feminism and anthropology. *Signs: Journal of Women in Culture and Society, 12,* 176-192.

Strauss, A. (1954). Strain and harmony in American-Japanese war bride marriages. *Journal of Marriage and Family Living, 16,* 99-106.

Sumida, S. H. (1996). *The power of place.* Paper presented at the 13th national conference of the Association for Asian American Studies, Washington, DC.

Sunoo, H. H., & Sunoo, S. S. (1976). The heritage of the first Korean women immigrants in the United States: 1903-1929. *Korean Christian Scholars Journal, 2,* 149-163.

Tajima, R. (1989). Lotus blossoms don't bleed: Images of Asian women. In Asian Women United of California (Ed.), *Making waves: An anthology of writings by and about Asian American women* (pp. 308-317). Boston: Beacon.

Tajima, R. (1991). Moving the image: Asian American independent filmmaking 1970-1990. In R. Leong (Ed.), *Moving the image: Independent Asian Pacific American media arts* (pp. 10-33). Los Angeles: University of California at Los Angeles, Asian American Studies Center, and Visual Communications, Southern California Asian American Studies Central.

Takaki, R. (1989). *Strangers from a different shore: A history of Asian Americans.* Boston: Little, Brown.

Tan, A. (1989). *The Joy Luck Club.* New York: Putnam's.

Tienda, M., & Booth, K. (1991). Gender, migration, and social change. *International Sociology, 6,* 51-72.

Tong, B. (1994). *Unsubmissive women: Chinese prostitutes in nineteenth-century San Francisco.* Norman: University of Oklahoma Press.

Tran, Q. P. (1993). Exile and home in contemporary Vietnamese American feminine writing. *Amerasia Journal, 19,* 71-83.

U.S. Bureau of the Census. (1992). *Statistical abstract of the United States: 1992* (112th ed.). Washington, DC: Government Printing Office.

U.S. Bureau of the Census. (1993). *We the American Asians.* Washington, DC: Government Printing Office.

Villanueva, M. (1991). *Ginseng and other tales from Manila.* Corvallis, OR: Calyx.

Villones, R. (1989). Women in the Silicon Valley. In Asian Women United of California (Ed.), *Making waves: An anthology of writings by and about Asian American women* (pp. 172-176). Boston: Beacon.

Wallovitts, S. E. (1972). *The Filipinos in California.* San Francisco: R&E Associates.

Wang, A. (1988). Maxine Hong Kingston's reclaiming of America: The birthright of the Chinese American male. *South Dakota Review, 26,* 18-29.

Weinberg, S. S. (1992). The treatment of women in immigration history: A call for change. In D. Gabaccia (Ed.), *Seeking common ground: Multidisciplinary studies of immigrant women in the United States* (pp. 3-22). Westport, CT: Greenwood.

Welaratna, U. (1993). *Beyond the killing fields: Voices of nine Cambodian survivors in America.* Stanford, CA: Stanford University Press.

Welaratna, U. (1993). *Beyond the killing fields: Voices of nine Cambodian survivors in America.* Stanford, CA: Stanford University Press.

Wiegman, R. (1991). Black bodies/American commodities: Gender, race, and the bourgeois ideal in contemporary film. In L. D. Friedman (Ed.), *Unspeakable images: Ethnicity and the American cinema* (pp. 308-328). Urbana: University of Illinois Press.

Williams, M. (1989). Ladies on the line: Punjabi cannery workers in central California. In Asian Women United of California (Ed.), *Making waves: An anthology of writings by and about Asian American women* (pp. 148-159). Boston: Beacon.

Wong, B. (1976). Life in a Chinese laundry: Interview with John Gee. In E. Gee (Ed.), *Counterpoint: Perspectives on Asian America* (pp. 338-344). Los Angeles: University of California at Los Angeles, Asian American Studies Center.

Wong, E. F. (1978). *On visual media racism: Asians in the American motion pictures.* New York: Arno.

Wong, M. (1980). Changes in socioeconomic status of the Chinese male population in the United States from 1960 to 1970. *International Migration Review, 14,* 511-524.

Wong, M. (1983). Chinese sweatshops in the United States: A look at the garment industry. *Research in Sociology of Work: Peripheral Workers, 2,* 357-379.

Wong, M. (1995). Chinese Americans. In P. G. Min (Ed.), *Asian Americans: Contemporary trends and issues* (pp. 58-94). Thousand Oaks, CA: Sage.

Wong, S.-L. C. (1992). Ethnicizing gender: An exploration of sexuality as sign in Chinese immigrant literature. In S. G. Lim & A. Ling (Eds.), *Reading the literatures of Asian America* (pp. 111-129). Philadelphia: Temple University Press.

Wong, S.-L. C. (1993). *Reading Asian American literature: From necessity to extravagance.* Princeton, NJ: Princeton University Press.

Wong, Y.-M. W. (1989). Behind unmarked doors: Developments in the garment industry. In Asian Women United of California (Ed.), *Making waves: An anthology of writings by and about Asian American women* (pp. 159-171). Boston: Beacon.

Woo, D. (1985). The socioeconomic status of Asian American women in the labor force: An alternative view. *Sociological Perspectives, 28,* 307-338.

Wu, W. F. (1982). *The Yellow Peril: Chinese Americans in American fiction 1850-1940.* Hamden, CT: Archon.

Yamanaka, K., & McClelland, K. (1994). Earning the model-minority image: Diverse strategies of economic adaptation by Asian-American women. *Ethnic and Racial Studies, 17,* 79-114.

Yamanaka, L. A. (1993). Empty heart. In J. Hagedorn (Ed.), *Charlie Chan is dead: An anthology of contemporary Asian American fiction* (pp. 544-550). New York: Penguin.

Yanagisako, S. (1995). Transforming orientalism: Gender, nationality, and class in Asian American studies. In S. Yanagisako & C. Delaney (Eds.), *Naturalizing power: Essays in feminist cultural analysis* (pp. 275-298). New York: Routledge.

Yanagisako, S. J. (1987). Mixed metaphors: Native and anthropological models of gender and kinship domains. In J. F. Collier & S. J. Yanagisako (Eds.), *Gender and kinship: Essays toward a unified analysis* (pp. 86-118). Stanford, CA: Stanford University Press.

Yang, E. S. (1987). Korean women in America: 1903-1930. In E.-Y. Yu & E. H. Philipps (Eds.), *Korean women in transition: At home and abroad* (pp. 167-181). Los Angeles: California State University, Center for Korean-American and Korean Studies.

Yim, S. B. (1989). Korean immigrant women in early twentieth-century America. In Asian Women United of California (Ed.), *Making waves: An anthology of writings by and about Asian American women* (pp. 50-59). Boston: Beacon.

Yoon, D. D. (1993, November 26). Asian American male: Wimp or what? *Asian Week*, p. 16.

Yu, C. Y. (1989). The world of our grandmothers. In Asian Women United of California (Ed.), *Making waves: An anthology of writings by and about Asian American women* (pp. 33-42). Boston: Beacon.

Yu, E.-Y. (1987). Korean-American women: Demographic profiles and family roles. In E.-Y. Yu & E. H. Phillips (Eds.), *Korean women in transition: At home and abroad* (pp. 183-197). Los Angeles: California State University, Center for Korean-American and Korean Studies.

Yu, H. (1995, November). *The spatialization of race: Chicago sociologists and the "Oriental problem."* Paper presented at the University of California, San Diego Urban Studies Colloquium Series, La Jolla.

Yung, J. (1986). *Chinese women of America: A pictorial essay.* Seattle: University of Washington Press.

Yung, J. (1990). *Unbinding the feet, unbinding their lives: Social change for Chinese women in San Francisco, 1902-1945.* Ph.D. dissertation, University of California, Berkeley.

Zhao, X. (in press). Chinese American women defense workers in World War II. *California History.*

Zhou, M., & Logan, J. R. (1989). Returns on human capital in ethnic enclaves: New York City's Chinatown. *American Sociological Review, 54,* 809-820.

About the Author

Yen Le Espiritu, Associate Professor of Ethnic Studies at the University of California, San Diego, has written on ethnicity, immigration, and race relations. Originally from Vietnam, she is the author of *Asian American Panethnicity: Bridging Institutions and Identities* and *Filipino American Lives.*